A PAGEANT OF
MODERN VERSE

A PAGEANT OF
MODERN VERSE

Selected by

E. W. PARKER, M.C.

LONGMANS

LONGMANS, GREEN AND CO LTD
6 & 7 CLIFFORD STREET, LONDON W I

THIBAULT HOUSE, THIBAULT SQUARE, CAPE TOWN
605–611 LONSDALE STREET, MELBOURNE C I
443 LOCKHART ROAD, HONG KONG
ACCRA, AUCKLAND, IBADAN
KINGSTON (JAMAICA), KUALA LUMPUR
LAHORE, NAIROBI, SALISBURY (RHODESIA)

LONGMANS, GREEN AND CO INC
I 19 WEST 40TH STREET, NEW YORK 18

LONGMANS, GREEN AND CO
20 CRANFIELD ROAD, TORONTO 16

ORIENT LONGMANS PRIVATE LTD
CALCUTTA, BOMBAY, MADRAS
DELHI, HYDERABAD, DACCA

First published 1949
Ninth Impression 1960

PRINTED IN GREAT BRITAIN BY
NEILL AND CO LTD EDINBURGH

FOREWORD

THIS selection from the works of the poets of our own time is the final part of *A Pageant of English Verse*.

It is hoped that it will serve both as an introduction to the finest work of our leading poets from Meredith to the present day and as an incentive to the reader to explore further among the vast number of collections of poetry, such as those listed in the "Acknowledgements" in this volume.

ACKNOWLEDGEMENTS

ACKNOWLEDGEMENT is due to the following for permission to use copyright material :—

Mrs Binyon, The Society of Authors and The Macmillan Company of New York for "For the Fallen" by Laurence Binyon; Mr Edmund Blunden for "The Idlers" from his *Poems*; Messrs Chatto & Windus for "Strange Meeting" from *Poems* by Wilfred Owen; Messrs J. M. Dent & Sons Ltd. for "The Praise of Dust" from *The Wild Knight and Other Poems* by G. K. Chesterton, and Messrs Methuen & Co. Ltd. and the author's executrix for "The Rolling English Road" from *Wine, Water and Song*, and "The Secret People" from *Collected Poems* by G. K. Chesterton; The Clarendon Press, Oxford, for "A Passer-by," "Nightingales," "The Winnowers" and "London Snow" from *Shorter Poems of Robert Bridges*; Mr Alex Comfort and Messrs Routledge and Kegan Paul Ltd. for "Third Elegy" from *Elegies*; Messrs Constable & Co. Ltd. for stanzas from *The Woods of Westermain* by George Meredith; Mr Walter de la Mare for "A Song of Enchantment" from *Peacock Pie*, and "Evening," "Music," "The Scarecrow," "The Moth," "The Scribe" and "Farewell" from *Collected Poems*, published by Faber & Faber Ltd.; Messrs J. M. Dent & Sons Ltd. and the author for "The Road" from *Journeys and Places* by Edwin Muir; Lady Desborough for "Into Battle" by Julian Grenfell; Messrs Gerald Duckworth & Co. Ltd. for "The South Country" and "Ha'nacker Mill" from *Sonnets and Verses* by Hilaire Belloc, and for "Mrs Hague" and "On the Coast of Coromandel" from *Satires and Poems* by Sir Osbert Sitwell; Messrs Faber & Faber Ltd. and the authors for "The Journey of the Magi" and "The Hollow Men" from *Poems 1909–1935* by T. S. Eliot, "The Serf" and "Autumn" from *Adamastor* by Roy Campbell, "Look, Stranger" and "O what is that Sound" from *Look, Stranger, and Other Poems* by W. H. Auden, "The Express" from *Poems* by Stephen Spender, "Snow" from *Poems* by Louis MacNeice; Messrs Martin Secker & Warburg Ltd. and the author's executors for "The Golden

viii   ACKNOWLEDGEMENTS

Journey to Samarkand" and "The Old Ships" from *Collected Poems of James Elroy Flecker*; Mr Wilfrid Gibson and Messrs Macmillan & Co. Ltd. for "The Ice-cart" from *Collected Poems 1905–1925* and "The Blue Peter" from *Islands*; The Trustees of the Hardy Estate and Messrs Macmillan & Co. Ltd. for "Men who march away," "Afterwards," "Snow in the Suburbs," "Beeny Cliff," "In Time of 'The Breaking of Nations'," and "Beyond the Last Lamp" from *Collected Poems of Thomas Hardy*; Messrs Wm. Heinemann Ltd. for "The Garden of Proserpine" from *Collected Poems of A. C. Swinburne*; Messrs Hollis & Carter Ltd. for "The Shepherdess" and "Renouncement" by Alice Meynell; The Oxford University Press and the poet's family for "Pied Beauty," "Inversnaid," "God's Grandeur," "The Habit of Perfection," "As Kingfishers catch fire," "Nothing is so beautiful as Spring" and "The Starlight Night" from *Poems of Gerard Manley Hopkins*; The Trustees of the Estate of the late A. E. Housman and Messrs Jonathan Cape Ltd. for "Bredon Hill" and "Loveliest of Trees" from *Collected Poems of A. E. Housman*; Mrs Frieda Lawrence and Messrs William Heinemann Ltd. for "Snake" from *Collected Poems of D. H. Lawrence*; Mr Cecil Day Lewis and The Hogarth Press Ltd. for "A Time to Dance" and "The Ecstatic"; Dr John Masefield, The Society of Authors and The Macmillan Company of New York for "Beauty," "The West Wind" and "The Seekers" (copyright 1912 and 1913 by The Macmillan Company), and "On Malvern Hill" and "On Eastnor Knoll" (copyright 1918 by John Masefield); Mrs Harold Monro for "Solitude" from *Strange Meetings* by Harold Monro; The Oxford University Press for "Upon Eckington Bridge" from *Poems* by Sir Arthur Quiller-Couch; The Hon. V. Sackville-West and Messrs Putnam & Co. Ltd. for an extract from *The Land*, published by William Heinemann Ltd.; Mr Siegfried Sassoon for "Morning Express" from *The Old Huntsman and Other Poems*, and for "Everyone Sang" from *War Poems*, both published by William Heinemann Ltd.; Mr Edward Shanks for "Swimmers" from *Poems* published by Macmillan & Co. Ltd.; Messrs Sidgwick & Jackson Ltd. for "The Soldier," "The Fish," "The Great Lover" and "The Old Vicarage, Grantchester" from *Collected Poems of Rupert Brooke*; "Moonlit Apples" from *Collected Poems of John Drinkwater*; "The Almswomen" and stanzas from "The Barn" from *The Waggoner and Other Poems* by

Edmund Blunden; Mr Martyn Skinner and Messrs Putnam & Co. Ltd. for "One Man, symbolic of his Native Land" from *Letters to Malaya*, III–IV; Mr James Stephens and Messrs Macmillan & Co. Ltd. for "In a Poppy Field," "The Shell," "The Fifteen Acres" and "The Goat Paths" from *Collected Poems*; Mrs Helen Thomas for "If I should ever by chance grow rich" from *Collected Poems of Edward Thomas* published by Faber & Faber Ltd.; Sir Francis Meynell for "The Hound of Heaven," "To a Snowflake" and "The Kingdom of God" by Francis Thompson; Mrs W. B. Yeats and Messrs Macmillan & Co. Ltd. for "The Song of the Wandering Aengus," "The Host of the Air," "Aedh wishes for the Cloths of Heaven," "When you are old," "The Wild Swans at Coole" and "The Stolen Child" from *Collected Poems of W. B. Yeats*.

The Compiler wishes to thank his friends for a number of valuable suggestions and criticisms.

CONTENTS

CONTENTS

CONTENTS

MODERN VERSE

GEORGE MEREDITH

1828-1909

Enter these Enchanted Woods

Enter these enchanted woods,
    You who dare.
Nothing harms beneath the leaves
More than waves a swimmer cleaves.
Toss your heart up with the lark,
Foot at peace with mouse and worm,
    Fair you fare.
Only at a dread of dark
Quaver, and they quit their form:
Thousand eyeballs under hoods
    Have you by the hair.
Enter these enchanted woods,
    You who dare.

Here the snake across your path
Stretches in his golden bath:
Mossy-footed squirrels leap
Soft as winnowing plumes of Sleep:
Yaffles on a chuckle skim
Low to laugh from branches dim:
Up the pine, where sits the star,
Rattles deep the moth-winged jar.
Each has business of his own;
But should you distrust a tone,
    Then beware.
Shudder all the haunted roods,
All the eyeballs under hoods
    Shroud you in their glare.
Enter these enchanted woods,
    You who dare. . . .

From *The Woods of Westermain*

yaffles = green woodpeckers.

CHRISTINA GEORGINA ROSSETTI

1830-94

Remember

Remember me when I am gone away,
  Gone far away into the silent land;
  When you can no more hold me by the hand,
Nor I half turn to go, yet turning stay.
Remember me when no more day by day
  You tell me of our future that you plann'd:
  Only remember me; you understand
It will be late to counsel then or pray.

Yet if you should forget me for a while
  And afterwards remember, do not grieve:
  For if the darkness and corruption leave
  A vestige of the thoughts that once I had,
Better by far you should forget and smile
  Than that you should remember and be sad.

ALGERNON CHARLES SWINBURNE

1837-1909

The Garden of Proserpine

Here, where the world is quiet,
  Here, where all trouble seems
Dead winds' and spent waves' riot
  In doubtful dreams of dreams;
I watch the green field growing
For reaping folk and sowing,
For harvest-time and mowing,
  A sleepy world of streams.

I am tired of tears and laughter,
  And men that laugh and weep
Of what may come hereafter
  For men that sow to reap:

I am weary of days and hours,
Blown buds of barren flowers,
Desires and dreams and powers
   And everything but sleep.

Here life has death for neighbour
   And far from eye or ear
Wan waves and wet winds labour,
   Weak ships and spirits steer;
They drive adrift, and whither
They wot not who make thither;
But no such winds blow hither,
   And no such things grow here.

No growth of moor or coppice,
   No heather-flower or vine,
But bloomless buds of poppies,
   Green grapes of Proserpine,
Pale beds of blowing rushes
Where no leaf blooms or blushes
Save this whereout she crushes
   For dead men deadly wine.

Pale, without name or number,
   In fruitless fields of corn,
They bow themselves and slumber
   All night till light is born;
And like a soul belated,
In hell and heaven unmated,
By cloud and mist abated
   Comes out of darkness morn.

Though one were strong as seven,
   He too with death shall dwell,
Nor wake with wings in heaven,
   Nor weep for pains in hell;

Though one were fair as roses,
His beauty clouds and closes;
And well though love reposes,
   In the end it is not well.

Pale, beyond porch and portal,
   Crowned with calm leaves, she stands
Who gathers all things mortal
   With cold immortal hands;
Her languid lips are sweeter
Than love's who fears to greet her
To men that mix and meet her
   From many times and lands.

She waits for each and other,
   She waits for all men born;
Forgets the earth her mother,
   The life of fruits and corn;
And spring and seed and swallow
Take wing for her and follow
Where summer song rings hollow
   And flowers are put to scorn.

There go the loves that wither,
   The old loves with wearier wings;
And all dead years draw thither,
   And all disastrous things;
Dead dreams of days forsaken,
Blind buds that snows have shaken,
Wild leaves that winds have taken,
   Red strays of ruined springs.

We are not sure of sorrow,
   And joy was never sure;
To-day will die to-morrow;
   Time stoops to no man's lure;

And love, grown faint and fretful,
With lips but half regretful
Sighs, and with eyes forgetful
　Weeps that no loves endure.

From too much love of living,
　From hope and fear set free,
We thank with brief thanksgiving
　Whatever gods may be
That no life lives for ever;
That dead men rise up never;
That even the weariest river
　Winds somewhere safe to sea.

Then star nor sun shall waken,
　Nor any change of light:
Nor sound of waters shaken,
　Nor any sound or sight:
Nor wintry leaves nor vernal,
Nor days nor things diurnal;
Only the sleep eternal
　In an eternal night.

THOMAS HARDY

1840–1928

Men who March Away

Song of the Soldiers

What of the faith and fire within us
　Men who march away
　Ere the barn-cocks say
　Night is growing gray,
Leaving all that here can win us;
What of the faith and fire within us
　Men who march away?

Is it a purblind prank, O think you,
　　Friend with the musing eye,
　　Who watch us stepping by
　　With doubt and dolorous sigh?
Can much pondering so hoodwink you!
Is it a purblind prank, O think you,
　　Friend with the musing eye?

Nay, we well see what we are doing
　　Though some may not see—
　　Dalliers as they be—
　　England's need are we;
Her distress would leave us rueing:
Nay, we well see what we are doing
　　Though some may not see!

In our heart of hearts believing
　　Victory crowns the just,
　　And that braggarts must
　　Surely bite the dust,
Press we to the field ungrieving,
In our heart of hearts believing
　　Victory crowns the just.

Hence the faith and fire within us
　　Men who march away
　　Ere the barn-cocks say
　　Night is growing gray,
Leaving all that here can win us;
Hence the faith and fire within us
　　Men who march away.

5th September 1914.

Afterwards

When the Present has latched its postern behind my tremulous
　　stay,
　　And the May month flaps its glad green leaves like wings,
Delicate-filmed as new-spun silk, will the neighbours say,
　　'He was a man who used to notice such things'?

If it be in the dusk when, like an eyelid's soundless blink,
  The dewfall-hawk comes crossing the shades to alight
Upon the wind-warped upland thorn, a gazer may think,
  'To him this must have been a familiar sight.'

If I pass during some nocturnal blackness, mothy and warm,
  When the hedgehog travels furtively over the lawn,
One may say, 'He strove that such innocent creatures should
    come to no harm,
  But he could do little for them; and now he is gone.'

If, when hearing that I have been stilled at last, they stand at
    the door,
  Watching the full-starred heavens that winter sees,
Will this thought rise on those who will meet my face no more,
  'He was one who had an eye for such mysteries'?

And will any say when my bell of quittance is heard in the
    gloom,
  And a crossing breeze cuts a pause in its outrollings,
Till they rise again, as they were a new bell's boom,
  'He hears it not now, but used to notice such things'?

Snow in the Suburbs

  Every branch big with it,
  Bent every twig with it;
Every fork like a white web-foot;
Every street and pavement mute:
Some flakes have lost their way, and grope back upward, when
Meeting those meandering down they turn and descend again.
  The palings are glued together like a wall,
  And there is no waft of wind with the fleecy fall.

                                          L*

A sparrow enters the tree,
Whereon immediately
A snow-lump thrice his own slight size
Descends on him and showers his head and eyes,
And overturns him,
And near inurns him,
And lights on a nether twig, when its brush
Starts off a volley of other lodging lumps with a rush.

The steps are a blanched slope,
Up which, with feeble hope,
A black cat comes, wide-eyed and thin;
And we take him in.

In Time of 'The Breaking of Nations'

Only a man harrowing clods
In a slow silent walk
With an old horse that stumbles and nods
Half asleep as they stalk.

Only thin smoke without flame
From the heaps of couch-grass;
Yet this will go onward the same
Though Dynasties pass.

Yonder a maid and her wight
Come whispering by;
War's annals will cloud into night
Ere their story die.

Beeny Cliff

O the opal and the sapphire of that wandering western sea,
And the woman riding high above with bright hair flapping
    free—
The woman whom I loved so, and who loyally loved me.

The pale mews plained below us, and the waves seemed far
    away
In a nether sky, engrossed in saying their ceaseless babbling
    say,
As we laughed light-heartedly aloft on that clear-sunned March
    day.

A little cloud then cloaked us, and there flew an irised rain,
And the Atlantic dyed its levels with a dull misfeatured stain,
And then the sun burst out again, and purples prinked the
    main.

—Still in all its chasmal beauty bulks old Beeny to the sky,
And shall she and I not go there once again now March is
    nigh,
And the sweet things said in that March say anew there by and
    by?

What if still in chasmal beauty looms that wild weird western
    shore,
The woman now is—elsewhere—whom the ambling pony
    bore,
And nor knows nor cares for Beeny, and will laugh there
    nevermore.

Beyond the Last Lamp

(Near Tooting Common)

While rain, with eve in partnership,
Descended darkly, drip, drip, drip,
Beyond the last lone lamp I passed
    Walking slowly, whispering sadly,
    Two linked loiterers, wan, downcast:
Some heavy thought constrained each face,
And blinded them to time and place.

GERARD MANLEY HOPKINS

The pair seemed lovers, yet absorbed
In mental scenes no longer orbed
By love's young rays.   Each countenance
    As it slowly, as it sadly
    Caught the lamplight's yellow glance,
Held in suspense a misery
At things which had been or might be.

When I retrod that watery way
Some hours beyond the droop of day,
Still I found pacing there the twain
    Just as slowly, just as sadly,
    Heedless of the night and rain.
One could but wonder who they were
And what wild woe detained them there.

Though thirty years of blur and blot
Have slid since I beheld that spot,
And saw in curious converse there
    Moving slowly, moving sadly
    That mysterious tragic pair,
Its olden look may linger on—
All but the couple; they have gone.

Whither? Who knows, indeed. . . . And yet
To me, when nights are weird and wet,
Without those comrades there at tryst
    Creeping slowly, creeping sadly,
    That lone lane does not exist.
There they seem brooding on their pain,
And will, while such a lane remain.

GERARD MANLEY HOPKINS

1844-89

The Habit of Perfection

Elected Silence, sing to me
And beat upon my whorlèd ear,
Pipe me to pastures still and be
The music that I care to hear.

Shape nothing, lips; be lovely-dumb:
It is the shut, the curfew sent
From there where all surrenders come
Which only makes you eloquent.

Be shellèd, eyes, with double dark
And find the uncreated light:
This ruck and reel which you remark
Coils, keeps, and teases simple sight.

Palate, the hutch of tasty lust,
Desire not to be rinsed with wine:
The can must be so sweet, the crust
So fresh that come in fasts divine!

Nostrils, your careless breath that spend
Upon the stir and keep of pride,
What relish shall the censers send
Along the sanctuary side!

O feel-of-primrose hands, O feet
That want the yield of plushy sward,
But you shall walk the golden street,
And you unhouse and house the Lord.

And Poverty, be thou the bride
And now the marriage feast begun,
And lily-coloured clothes provide
Your spouse not laboured-at, nor spun.

God's Grandeur

The world is charged with the grandeur of God.
   It will flame out, like shining from shook foil;
   It gathers to a greatness, like the ooze of oil
Crushed. Why do men then now not reck his rod?
Generations have trod, have trod, have trod;
   And all is seared with trade; bleared, smeared with toil;
   And wears man's smudge and shares man's smell: the soil
Is bare now, nor can foot feel, being shod.

And for all this, nature is never spent;
  There lives the dearest freshness deep down things;
And though the last lights off the black West went
  Oh, morning, at the brown brink eastward, springs—
Because the Holy Ghost over the bent
  World broods with warm breast and with ah! bright wings.

As Kingfishers catch fire

As kingfishers catch fire, dragonflies dràw flàme;
As tumbled over rim in roundy wells
Stones ring; like each tucked string tells, each hung bell's
Bow swung finds tongue to fling out broad its name;
Each mortal thing does one thing and the same:
Deals out that being indoors each one dwells;
Selves—goes itself; *myself* it speaks and spells,
Crying *Whàt I do is me: for that I came.*

Ì say mòre: the just man justices;
Kèeps gràce: thàt keeps all his goings graces;
Acts in God's eye what in God's eye he is—
Chrìst—for Christ plays in ten thousand places,
Lovely in limbs, and lovely in eyes not his
To the Father through the features of men's faces.

Pied Beauty

Glory be to God for dappled things—
  For skies of couple-colour as a brinded cow;
    For rose-moles all in stipple upon trout that swim;
Fresh-firecoal chestnut-falls; finches' wings;
  Landscape plotted and pieced—fold, fallow, and plough;
    And àll tràdes, their gear and tackle and trim.

All things counter, original, spare, strange;
  Whatever is fickle, freckled (who knows how?)
    With swift, slow; sweet, sour; adazzle, dim;
He fathers-forth whose beauty is past change:
        Praise him.

Spring

Nothing is so beautiful as spring—
   When weeds, in wheels, shoot long and lovely and lush;
   Thrush's eggs look little low heavens, and thrush
Through the echoing timber does so rinse and wring
The ear, it strikes like lightnings to hear him sing;
   The glassy pear-tree leaves and blooms, they brush
   The descending blue; that blue is all in a rush
With richness; the racing lambs too have fair their fling.

What is all this juice and all this joy?
   A strain of the earth's sweet being in the beginning
In Eden garden.—Have, get, before it cloy,
   Before it cloud, Christ, lord, and sour with sinning,
Innocent mind and Mayday in girl and boy,
   Most, O maid's child, thy choice and worthy the winning.

Inversnaid

This darksome burn, horseback brown,
His roll rock highroad roaring down,
In coop and in comb the fleece of his foam
Flutes and low to the lake falls home.

A windpuff-bonnet of fàwn-fròth
Turns and twindles over the broth
Of a pool so pitch-black, fèll-fròwning
It rounds and rounds Despair to drowning.

Degged with dew, dappled with dew
Are the groins of the braes that the brook treads through,
Wiry heathpacks, flitches of fern,
And the beadbonny ash that sits over the burn.

What would the world be, once bereft
Of wet and wildness? Let them be left,
O let them be left, wildness and wet;
Long live the weeds and the wilderness yet.

The Starlight Night

Look at the stars! look, look up at the skies!
  O look at all the fire-folk sitting in the air!
  The bright boroughs, the circle-citadels there!
Down in dim woods the diamond delves! the elves'-eyes!
The grey lawns cold where gold, where quickgold lies!
  Wind-beat whitebeam! airy abeles set on a flare!
  Flake-doves sent floating forth at a farmyard scare!—
Ah well! it is all a purchase, all is a prize.

Buy then! bid then!—What?—Prayer, patience, alms, vows.
Look, look: a May-mess, like on orchard boughs!
  Look! March-bloom, like on mealed-with-yellow sallows!

These are indeed the barn; withindoors house
The shocks. This piece-bright paling shuts the spouse
  Christ home, Christ and his mother and all his hallows.

ROBERT BRIDGES

1844-1930

London Snow

When men were all asleep the snow came flying,
  In large white flakes falling on the city brown,
Stealthily and perpetually settling and loosely lying,
  Hushing the latest traffic of the drowsy town;
Deadening, muffling, stifling its murmurs failing;
Lazily and incessantly floating down and down:
  Silently sifting and veiling road, roof and railing;
Hiding difference, making unevenness even,
Into angles and crevices softly drifting and sailing.
  All night it fell, and when full inches seven
It lay in the depth of its uncompacted lightness,
The clouds blew off from a high and frosty heaven;
  And all woke earlier for the unaccustomed brightness

Of the winter dawning, the strange unheavenly glare:
The eye marvelled—marvelled at the dazzling whiteness;
  The ear hearkened to the stillness of the solemn air;
No sound of wheel rumbling nor of foot falling,
And the busy morning cries came thin and spare.
  Then boys I heard, as they went to school, calling,
They gathered up the crystal manna to freeze
Their tongues with tasting, their hands with snowballing;
  Or rioted in a drift, plunging up to the knees;
Or peering up from under the white-mossed wonder,
'O look at the trees!' they cried, 'O look at the trees!'
  With lessened load a few carts creak and blunder,
Following along the white deserted way,
A country company long dispersed asunder:
  When now already the sun, in pale display
Standing by Paul's high dome, spread forth below
His sparkling beams, and awoke the stir of the day.
  For now doors open, and war is waged with the snow;
And trains of sombre men, past tale of number,
Tread long brown paths, as toward their toil they go;
  But even for them awhile no cares encumber
Their minds diverted; the daily word is unspoken,
  The daily thoughts of labour and sorrow slumber
At the sight of the beauty that greets them, for the charm
    they have broken.

The Winnowers

Betwixt two billows of the downs
  The little hamlet lies,
And nothing sees but the bald crowns
  Of the hills, and the blue skies.

Clustering beneath the long descent
  And grey slopes of the wold,
The red roofs nestle, oversprent
  With lichen yellow as gold.

We found it in the mid-day sun
   Basking, what time of year
The thrush his singing has begun,
   Ere the first leaves appear.

High from his load a woodman pitched
   His faggots on the stack:
Knee-deep in straw the cattle twitched
   Sweet hay from crib and rack:

And from the barn hard by was borne
   A steady muffled din,
By which we knew that threshèd corn
   Was winnowing, and went in.

The sunbeams on the motey air
   Streamed through the open door,
And on the brown arms moving bare,
   And the grain upon the floor.

One turns the crank, one stoops to feed
   The hopper, lest it lack,
One in the bushel scoops the seed,
   One stands to hold the sack.

We watched the good grain rattle down,
   And the awns fly in the draught;
To see us both so pensive grown
   The honest labourers laughed:

Merry they were, because the wheat
   Was clean and plump and good,
Pleasant to hand and eye, and meet
   For market and for food.

It chanced we from the city were,
   And had not gat us free
In spirit from the store and stir
   Of its immensity:

But here we found ourselves again.
　Where humble harvests bring
After much toil but little grain,
　'Tis merry winnowing.

Nightingales

Beautiful must be the mountains whence ye come,
　And bright in the fruitful valleys the streams, wherefrom
　　　Ye learn your song:
Where are those starry woods? O might I wander there,
　Among the flowers, which in that heavenly air
　　　Bloom the year long!

Nay, barren are those mountains and spent the streams:
　Our song is the voice of desire, that haunts our dreams,
　　　A throe of the heart,
Whose pining visions dim, forbidden hopes profound,
　No dying cadence nor long sigh can sound,
　　　For all our art.

Alone, aloud in the raptured ear of men
　We pour our dark nocturnal secret; and then,
　　　As night is withdrawn
From these sweet-springing meads and bursting boughs of May,
　Dream, while the innumerable choir of day
　　　Welcome the dawn.

A Passer-by

Whither, O splendid ship, thy white sails crowding,
　Leaning across the bosom of the urgent West,
That fearest nor sea rising, nor sky clouding,
　Whither away, fair rover, and what thy quest?
　Ah! soon, when Winter has all our vales opprest,
When skies are cold and misty, and hail is hurling,
　Wilt thòu glide on the blue Pacific, or rest
In a summer haven asleep, thy white sails furling.

I there before thee, in the country that well thou knowest,
  Already arrived am inhaling the odorous air:
I watch thee enter unerringly where thou goest,
  And anchor queen of the strange shipping there,
  Thy sails for awnings spread, thy masts bare;
Nor is aught from the foaming reef to the snow-capped, grandest
  Peak, that is over the feathery palms more fair
Than thou, so upright, so stately, and still thou standest.

And yet, O splendid ship, unhailed and nameless,
  I know not if, aiming a fancy, I rightly divine
That thou hast a purpose joyful, a courage blameless,
  Thy port assured in a happier land than mine.
  But for all I have given thee, beauty enough is thine,
As thou, aslant with trim tackle and shrouding,
  From the proud nostril curve of a prow's line
In the offing scatterest foam, thy white sails crowding.

ALICE MEYNELL

1847-1922

The Shepherdess

She walks—the lady of my delight—
  A shepherdess of sheep.
Her flocks are thoughts.   She keeps them white;
  She guards them from the steep.
She feeds them on the fragrant height,
  And folds them in for sleep.

She roams maternal hills and bright,
  Dark valleys safe and deep.
Her dreams are innocent at night;
  The chastest stars may peep.
She walks—the lady of my delight—
  A shepherdess of sheep.

She holds her little thoughts in sight,
    Though gay they run and leap.
She is so circumspect and right;
    She has her soul to keep.
She walks—the lady of my delight—
    A shepherdess of sheep.

Renouncement

I must not think of thee; and, tired yet strong,
I shun the love that lurks in all delight—
The love of thee—and in the blue Heaven's height,
And in the sweetest passage of a song.
Oh, just beyond the fairest thoughts that throng
This breast, the thought of thee waits hidden yet bright;
But it must never, never come in sight;
I must stop short of thee the whole day long.
But when sleep comes to close each difficult day,
When night gives pause to the long watch I keep,
And all my bonds I needs must loose apart,
Must doff my will as raiment laid away.—
With the first dream that comes with the first sleep
I run, I run, I am gathered to thy heart.

ROBERT LOUIS STEVENSON

1850-94

In the Highlands

In the highlands, in the country places,
    Where the old plain men have rosy faces,
        And the young fair maidens
            Quiet eyes;
Where essential silence cheers and blesses,
And for ever in the hill-recesses
    Her more lovely music
        Broods and dies.

O to mount again where erst I haunted;
  Where the old red hills are bird-enchanted,
    And the low green meadows
      Bright with sward;
And when even dies, the million-tinted,
And the night has come, and planets glinted,
    Lo! the valley hollow,
      Lamp-bestarr'd.

O to dream, O to awake and wander
  There, and with delight to take and render,
    Through the trance of silence,
      Quiet breath!
Lo! for there, among the flowers and grasses,
Only the mightier movement sounds and passes;
    Only winds and rivers,
      Life and death.

Requiem

Under the wide and starry sky,
  Dig the grave and let me lie.
Glad did I live and gladly die,
  And I laid me down with a will.

This be the verse you grave for me:
Here he lies where he long'd to be;
Home is the sailor, home from sea,
  And the hunter home from the hill.

FRANCIS THOMPSON

1859-1907

To a Snowflake

What heart could have thought you?—
Past our devisal
(O filigree petal!)
Fashioned so purely,
Fragilely, surely,

From what Paradisal
Imagineless metal,
Too costly for cost?
Who hammered you, wrought you,
From argentine vapour?—
'God was my shaper.
Passing surmisal,
He hammered, He wrought me,
From curled silver vapour,
To lust of His mind:—
Thou couldst not have thought me!
So purely, so palely,
Tinily, surely,
Mightily, frailly,
Insculped and embossed,
With His hammer of wind,
And His graver of frost.'

The Kingdom of God

'*In No Strange Land*'

O world invisible, we view thee,
  O world intangible, we touch thee,
O world unknowable, we know thee,
  Inapprehensible, we clutch thee!

Does the fish soar to find the ocean,
  The eagle plunge to find the air—
That we ask of the stars in motion
  If they have rumour of thee there?

Not where the wheeling systems darken,
  And our benumbed conceiving soars!—
The drift of pinions, would we hearken,
  Beats at our own clay-shuttered doors.

The angels keep their ancient places;—
  Turn but a stone, and start a wing!
'Tis ye, 'tis your estrangèd faces,
  That miss the many-splendoured thing.

But (when so sad thou canst not sadder)
  Cry;—and upon thy so sore loss
Shall shine the traffic of Jacob's ladder
  Pitched betwixt Heaven and Charing Cross.

Yea, in the night, my Soul, my daughter,
  Cry,—clinging Heaven by the hems;
And lo, Christ walking on the water
  Not of Gennesareth, but Thames!

The Hound of Heaven

I fled him, down the nights and down the days;
  I fled Him, down the arches of the years;
I fled Him, down the labyrinthine ways
  Of my own mind; and in the midst of tears
I hid from Him, and under running laughter.
        Up vistaed hopes, I sped;
        And shot, precipitated,
  Adown Titanic glooms of chasmed fears,
  From those strong Feet that followed, followed after.
        But with unhurrying chase,
        And unperturbèd pace,
  Deliberate speed, majestic instancy,
        They beat—and a Voice beat
        More instant than the Feet—
  'All things betray thee, who betrayest Me.'

        I pleaded, outlaw-wise,
By many a hearted casement, curtained red,
  Trellised with intertwining charities;
(For, though I knew His love Who followèd,
        Yet was I sore adread
Lest, having Him, I must have naught beside.)
But, if one little casement parted wide,
  The gust of His approach would clash it to:
  Fear wist not to evade, as Love wist to pursue.
Across the margent of the world I fled,

And troubled the gold gateways of the stars,
Smiting for shelter on their clangèd bars;
    Fretted to dulcet jars
And silvern clatter the pale ports o' the moon.
I said to Dawn: Be sudden—to Eve: Be soon—
  With thy young skiey blossoms heap me over
    From this tremendous Lover!

Float thy vague veil about me, lest He see!
  I tempted all His servitors, but to find
My own betrayal in their constancy,
In faith to Him their fickleness to me,
  Their traitorous trueness, and their loyal deceit,
To all swift things for swiftness did I sue;
  Clung to the whistling mane of every wind.
    But whether they swept, smoothly fleet,
    The long savannahs of the blue;
    Or whether, Thunder-driven,
    They clanged his chariot 'thwart a heaven,
Plashy with flying lightnings round the spurn o' their feet:—
  Fear wist not to evade as Love wist to pursue.
    Still with unhurrying chase,
    And unperturbèd pace,
  Deliberate speed, majestic instancy,
    Came on the following Feet,
    And a Voice above their beat—
'Naught shelters thee, who wilt not shelter Me.'

I sought no more that after which I strayed
    In face of man or maid;
But still within the little children's eyes
    Seems something, something that replies,
They at least are for me, surely for me!
I turned me to them very wistfully;
But just as their young eyes grew sudden fair
    With dawning answers there,
Their angel plucked them from me by the hair.
'Come then, ye other children, Nature's—share
With me' (said I) 'your delicate fellowship;

Let me greet you lip to lip,
Let me twine with you caresses,
    Wantoning
With our Lady-Mother's vagrant tresses,
    Banqueting
With her in her wind-walled palace,
Underneath her azured daïs,
Quaffing, as your taintless way is,
    From a chalice
Lucent-weeping out of the dayspring.'
    So it was done:
I in their delicate fellowship was one—
Drew the bolt of Nature's secrecies.
    I knew all the swift importings
    On the wilful face of skies;
    I knew how the clouds arise
    Spumèd of the wild sea-snortings;
    All that's born or dies
Rose and drooped with; made them shapers
Of mine own moods, or wailful or divine;
    With them joyed and was bereaven.
    I was heavy with the even,
When she lit her glimmering tapers
Round the day's dead sanctities.
I laughed in the morning's eyes.
I triumphed and I saddened with all weather,
    Heaven and I wept together,
And its sweet tears were salt with mortal mine;
Against the red throb of its sunset-heart
    I laid my own to beat,
    And share commingling heat;
But not by that, by that, was eased my human smart.
In vain my tears were wet on Heaven's grey cheek.
For ah! we know not what each other says,
    These things and I; in sound *I* speak—
Their sound is but their stir, they speak by silences.
Nature, poor stepdame, cannot slake my drouth;
    Let her, if she would owe me,
Drop yon blue bosom-veil of sky, and show me
    The breasts o' her tenderness:

Never did any milk of hers once bless
        My thirsting mouth.
        Nigh and nigh draws the chase,
        With unperturbèd pace,
    Deliberate speed, majestic instancy,
        And past those noisèd Feet
        A Voice comes yet more fleet—
  'Lo! naught contents thee, who content'st not Me.'

Naked I wait Thy love's uplifted stroke!
My harness piece by piece Thou hast hewn from me,
        And smitten me to my knee;
        I am defenceless utterly.
        I slept, methinks, and woke,
And, slowly gazing, find me stripped in sleep.
In the rash lustihead of my young powers,
        I shook the pillaring hours
And pulled my life upon me; grimed with smears,
I stand amid the dust o' the mounded years—
My mangled youth lies dead beneath the heap.
My days have crackled and gone up in smoke,
Have puffed and burst as sun-starts on a stream.
        Yea, faileth now even dream
  The dreamer, and the lute the lutanist;
Even the linked fantasies, in whose blossomy twist
I swung the earth a trinket at my wrist,
Are yielding; cords of all too weak account
For earth with heavy griefs so overplussed.
        Ah! is Thy love indeed
A weed, albeit an amaranthine weed,
Suffering no flowers except its own to mount?
        Ah! must—
        Designer infinite!—
Ah! must Thou char the wood ere Thou canst limn with it?
My freshness spent its wavering shower i' the dust;
And now my heart is as a broken fount,
Wherein tear-drippings stagnate, spilt down ever
        From the dank thoughts that shiver
Upon the sighful branches of my mind.
        Such is; what is to be?
  The pulp so bitter, how shall taste the rind?

I dimly guess what Time in mists confounds;
Yet ever and anon a trumpet sounds
From the hid battlements of Eternity,
Those shaken mists a space unsettle, then
Round the half-glimpsèd turrets slowly wash again;
      But not ere him who summoneth
      I first have seen, enwound
With glooming robes purpureal, cypress-crowned;
His name I know, and what his trumpet saith.
Whether man's heart or life it be which yields
      Thee harvest, must Thy harvest fields
      Be dunged with rotten death?

      Now of that long pursuit
      Comes on at hand the bruit;
That Voice is round me like a bursting sea:
      'And is thy earth so marred,
      Shattered in shard on shard?
Lo, all things fly thee, for thou fliest Me!

      ' Strange, piteous, futile thing!
Wherefore should any set thee love apart?
Seeing none but I makes much of naught' (He said),
'And human love needs human meriting:
      How hast thou merited—
Of all man's clotted clay the dingiest clot?
      Alack, thou knowest not
How little worthy of any love thou art!
Whom wilt thou find to love ignoble thee,
      Save Me, save only Me?
All which I took from thee I did but take,
      Not for thy harms,
But just that thou might'st seek it in My arms.
      All which thy child's mistake
Fancies as lost, I have stored for thee at home:
      Rise, clasp My hand, and come.'
      Halts by me that footfall:
      Is my gloom, after all,
Shade of His hand, outstretched caressingly?
      'Ah, fondest, blindest, weakest,
      I am He Whom thou seekest!
Thou dravest love from thee, who dravest me.'

ALFRED EDWARD HOUSMAN

1859-1936

Bredon Hill

In summertime on Bredon
  The bells they sound so clear;
Round both the shires they ring them
  In steeples far and near,
  A happy noise to hear.

Here of a Sunday morning
  My love and I would lie,
And see the coloured counties,
  And hear the larks so high
  About us in the sky.

The bells would ring to call her
  In valleys miles away:
'Come all to church, good people;
  Good people, come and pray.'
  But here my love would stay.

And I would turn and answer
  Among the springing thyme,
'Oh, peal upon our wedding,
  And we will hear the chime,
  And come to church in time.'

But when the snows at Christmas
  On Bredon top were strown,
My love rose up so early
  And stole out unbeknown
  And went to church alone.

They tolled the one bell only,
  Groom there was none to see,
The mourners followed after,
  And so to church went she,
  And would not wait for me.

The bells they sound on Bredon,
  And still the steeples hum.
'Come all to church, good people,'—
  Oh, noisy bells, be dumb;
  I hear you, I will come.

Loveliest of Trees

Loveliest of trees, the cherry now
Is hung with bloom along the bough,
And stands about the woodland ride
Wearing white for Eastertide.

Now, of my threescore years and ten,
Twenty will not come again,
And take from seventy springs a score,
It only leaves me fifty more.

And since to look at things in bloom
Fifty springs are little room,
About the woodlands I will go
To see the cherry hung with snow.

WILLIAM BUTLER YEATS

1865-19

The Stolen Child

Where dips the rocky highland
Of Sleuth Wood in the lake,
There lies a leafy island
Where flapping herons wake
The drowsy water-rats;
There we've hid our faery vats,
Full of berries,
And of the reddest stolen cherries.

Come away, O human child!
To the waters and the wild
With a faery, hand in hand,
For the world's more full of weeping than you can understand.

Where the wave of moonlight glosses
The dim gray sands with light,
Far off by furthest Rosses
We foot it all the night,
Weaving olden dances,
Mingling hands and mingling glances
Till the moon has taken flight;
To and fro we leap
And chase the frothy bubbles,
While the world is full of troubles
And is anxious in its sleep.
Come away, O human child!
To the waters and the wild
With a faery, hand in hand,
For the world's more full of weeping than you can understand.

Where the wandering water gushes
From the hills above Glen-Car,
In pools among the rushes
That scarce could bathe a star,
We seek for slumbering trout
And, whispering in their ears,
Give them unquiet dreams;
Leaning softly out
From ferns that drop their tears
Over the young streams.
Come away, O human child!
To the waters and the wild
With a faery, hand in hand,
For the world's more full of weeping than you can understand.

Away with us he's going,
The solemn-eyed:
He'll hear no more the lowing
Of the calves on the warm hillside;

Or the kettle on the hob
Sing peace into his breast,
Or see the brown mice bob
Round and round the oatmeal-chest.
For he comes, the human child,
To the waters and the wild
With a faery, hand in hand,
From a world more full of weeping than he can understand.

Aedh wishes for the Cloths of Heaven

Had I the heavens' embroidered cloths,
  Enwrought with golden and silver light,
The blue and the dim and the dark cloths
  Of night and light and the half light,
I would spread the cloths under your feet:
  But I, being poor, have only my dreams;
I have spread my dreams under your feet;
  Tread softly because you tread on my dreams.

The Wild Swans at Coole

The trees are in their autumn beauty,
The woodland paths are dry,
Under the October twilight the water
Mirrors a still sky;
Upon the brimming water among the stones
Are nine-and-fifty swans.

The nineteenth Autumn has come upon me
Since I first made my count;
I saw, before I had well finished,
All suddenly mount
And scatter wheeling in great broken rings
Upon their clamorous wings.

I have looked upon those brilliant creatures,
And now my heart is sore.
All's changed since I, hearing at twilight,
The first time on this shore,
The bell-beat of their wings above my head,
Trod with a lighter tread.

Unwearied still, lover by lover,
They paddle in the cold
Companionable streams or climb the air;
Their hearts have not grown old;
Passion or conquest, wander where they will,
Attend upon them still.

But now they drift on the still water,
Mysterious, beautiful;
Among what rushes will they build,
By what lake's edge or pool
Delight men's eyes when I awake some day
To find they have flown away?

When You are Old

When you are old and gray and full of sleep,
    And nodding by the fire, take down this book,
    And slowly read, and dream of the soft look
Your eyes had once, and of their shadows deep;

How many loved your moments of glad grace,
    And loved your beauty with love false or true,
    But one man loved the pilgrim soul in you,
And loved the sorrows of your changing face;

And bending down beside the glowing bars,
    Murmur, a little sadly, how Love fled
    And paced upon the mountains overhead
And hid his face amid a crowd of stars.

M

The Host of the Air

O'Driscoll drove with a song
The wild duck and the drake
From the tall and the tufted reeds
Of the drear Hart Lake.

And he saw how the reeds grew dark
At the coming of night-tide,
And dreamed of the long dim hair
Of Bridget his bride.

He heard while he sang and dreamed
A piper piping away,
And never was piping so sad,
And never was piping so gay.

And he saw young men and young girls
Who danced on a level place,
And Bridget his bride among them,
With a sad and a gay face.

The dancers crowded about him,
And many a sweet thing said,
And a young man brought him red wine
And a young girl white bread.

And Bridget drew him by the sleeve,
Away from the merry bands,
To old men playing at cards
With a twinkling of ancient hands.

The bread and the wine had a doom,
For these were the host of the air;
He sat and played in a dream
Of her long dim hair.

He played with the merry old men
And thought not of evil chance,
Until one bore Bridget his bride
Away from the merry dance.

He bore her away in his arms,
The handsomest young man there,
And his neck and his breast and his arms
Were drowned in her long dim hair.

O'Driscoll scattered the cards
And out of his dream awoke:
Old men and young men and young girls
Were gone like a drifting smoke;

But he heard high up in the air
A piper piping away,
And never was piping so sad,
And never was piping so gay.

The Song of the Wandering Aengus

I went out to the hazel wood,
Because a fire was in my head,
And cut and peeled a hazel wand,
And hooked a berry to a thread;
And when white moths were on the wing,
And moth-like stars were flickering out,
I dropped the berry in a stream
And caught a little silver trout.

When I had laid it on the floor
I went to blow the fire a-flame,
But something rustled on the floor,
And some one called me by my name:
It had become a glimmering girl
With apple blossom in her hair
Who called me by my name and ran
And faded through the brightening air.

Though I am old with wandering
Through hollow lands and hilly lands,
I will find out where she has gone,
And kiss her lips and take her hands;
And walk among long dappled grass,
And pluck till time and times are done
The silver apples of the moon,
The golden apples of the sun.

LAURENCE BINYON

1869-1943

For the Fallen

With proud thanksgiving, a mother for her children,
England mourns for her dead across the sea.
Flesh of her flesh they were, spirit of her spirit,
Fallen in the cause of the free.

Solemn the drums thrill: Death august and royal
Sings sorrow up into immortal spheres.
There is music in the midst of desolation
And a glory that shines upon our tears.

They went with songs to the battle, they were young,
Straight of limb, true of eye, steady and aglow.
They were staunch to the end against odds uncounted,
They fell with their faces to the foe.

They shall grow not old, as we that are left grow old:
Age shall not weary them, nor the years condemn.
At the going down of the sun and in the morning
We will remember them.

They mingle not with their laughing comrades again;
They sit no more at familiar tables of home;
They have no lot in our labour of the day-time;
They sleep beyond England's foam.

But where our desires are and our hopes profound,
Felt as a well-spring that is hidden from sight,
To the innermost heart of their own land they are known
As the stars are known to the Night.

As the stars that shall be bright when we are dust,
Moving in marches upon the heavenly plain,
As the stars that are starry in the time of our darkness,
To the end, to the end, they remain.

HILAIRE BELLOC

b. 1870

The South Country

When I am living in the Midlands,
  That are sodden and unkind,
I light my lamp in the evening:
  My work is left behind;
And the great hills of the South Country
  Come back into my mind.

The great hills of the South Country
  They stand along the sea,
And it's there walking in the high woods
  That I could wish to be,
And the men that were boys when I was a boy
  Walking along with me.

The men that live in North England
  I saw them for a day:
Their hearts are set upon the waste fells,
  Their skies are fast and grey;
From their castle-walls a man may see
  The mountains far away.

The men that live in West England
  They see the Severn strong,
A-rolling on rough water brown
  Light aspen leaves along.
They have the secret of the Rocks
  And the oldest kind of song.

But the men that live in the South Country
   Are the kindest and most wise,
They get their laughter from the loud surf,
   And the faith in their happy eyes
Comes surely from our Sister the Spring
   When over the sea she flies;
The violets suddenly bloom at her feet,
   She blesses us with surprise.

I never get between the pines
   But I smell the Sussex air;
Nor I never come on a belt of sand
   But my home is there.
And along the sky the line of the Downs
   So noble and so bare.

A lost thing could I never find,
   Nor a broken thing mend:
And I fear I shall be all alone
   When I get towards the end.
Who will there be to comfort me
   Or who will be my friend?

I will gather and carefully make my friends
   Of the men of the Sussex Weald,
They watch the stars from silent folds,
   They stiffly plough the field.
By them and the God of the South Country
   My poor soul shall be healed.

If I ever become a rich man,
   Or if ever I grow to be old,
I will build a house with deep thatch
   To shelter me from the cold,
And there shall the Sussex songs be sung
   And the story of Sussex told.

I will hold my house in the high wood,
   Within a walk of the sea,
And the men that were boys when I was a boy
   Shall sit and drink with me.

Ha'nacker Mill

Sally is gone that was so kindly
  Sally is gone from Ha'nacker Hill.
And the Briar grows ever since then so blindly
  And ever since then the clapper is still,
  And the sweeps have fallen from Ha'nacker Mill.

Ha'nacker Hill is in Desolation:
  Ruin a-top and a field unploughed.
And Spirits that call on a falling nation
  Spirits that loved her calling aloud:
  Spirits abroad in a windy cloud.

Spirits that call and no one answers;
  Ha'nacker's down and England's done.
Wind and Thistle for pipe and dancers
  And never a ploughman under the Sun.
  Never a ploughman. Never a one.

WALTER DE LA MARE

1873-1956

The Scribe

What lovely things
Thy hand hath made:
The smooth-plumed bird
In its emerald shade,
The seed of the grass,
The speck of stone
Which the wayfaring ant
Stirs—and hastes on!

Though I should sit
By some tarn in thy hills,
Using its ink
As the spirit wills
To write of Earth's wonders,

Its live, willed things,
Flit would the ages
On soundless wings
Ere unto Z
My pen drew nigh;
Leviathan told,
And the honey-fly:
And still would remain
My wit to try—
My worn reeds broken
The dark tarn dry,
All words forgotten—
Thou, Lord, and I.

Music

When music sounds, gone is the earth I know,
And all her lovely things even lovelier grow;
Her flowers in vision flame, her forest trees
Lift burdened branches, stilled with ecstasies.

When music sounds, out of the water rise
Naiads whose beauty dims my waking eyes,
Rapt in strange dream burns each enchanted face,
With solemn echoing stirs their dwelling-place.

When music sounds, all that I was I am
Ere to this haunt of brooding dust I came;
While from Time's woods break into distant song
The swift-winged hours, as I hasten along.

Evening

When twilight darkens, and one by one,
The sweet birds to their nests have gone;
When to green banks the glow-worms bring
Pale lamps to brighten evening;
Then stirs in his thick sleep the owl,
Through the dewy air to prowl.

Hawking the meadow, swiftly he flits,
While the small mouse a-trembling sits
With tiny eye of fear upcast
Until his brooding shape be past,
Hiding her where the moonbeams beat,
Casting black shadows in the wheat.

Now all is still: the field-man is
Lapped deep in slumbering silentness.
Not a leaf stirs, but clouds on high
Pass in dim flocks across the sky,
Puffed by a breeze too light to move
Aught but these wakeful sheep above.

O, what an arch of light now spans
These fields by night no longer Man's!
Their ancient Master is abroad,
Walking beneath the moonlight cold:
His presence is the stillness, He
Fills earth with wonder and mystery.

The Moth

Isled in the midnight air,
Musked with the dark's faint bloom,
Out into glooming and secret haunts
   The flame cries, 'Come!'

Lovely in dye and fan,
A-tremble in shimmering grace,
A moth from her winter swoon
   Uplifts her face:

Stares from her glamorous eyes;
Wafts her on plumes like mist;
In ecstasy swirls and sways
   To her strange tryst.

M *

The Scarecrow

All winter through I bow my head
  Beneath the driving rain;
The North wind powders me with snow
  And blows me black again;
At midnight in a maze of stars
  I flame with glittering rime,
And stand, above the stubble, stiff
  As mail at morning-prime.
But when that child, called Spring, and all
  His host of children, come,
Scattering their buds and dew upon
  These acres of my home,
Some rapture in my rags awakes;
  I lift void eyes and scan
The skies for crows, those ravening foes,
  Of my strange master, Man.
I watch him striding lank behind
  His clashing team, and know
Soon will the wheat swish body high
  Where once lay sterile snow;
Soon shall I gaze across a sea
  Of sun-begotten grain,
Which my unflinching watch hath sealed
  For harvest once again.

Fare Well

When I lie where shades of darkness
Shall no more assail mine eyes,
Nor the rain make lamentation
  When the wind sighs;
How will fare the world whose wonder
Was the very proof of me?
Memory fades, must the remembered
  Perishing be?

Oh, when this my dust surrenders
Hand, foot, lip, to dust again,
May those loved and loving faces
        Please other men!
May the rusting harvest hedgerow
Still the Traveller's Joy entwine,
And as happy children gather
        Posies once mine.

Look thy last on all things lovely,
Every hour.   Let no night
Seal thy sense in deathly slumber
        Till to delight
Thou have paid thy utmost blessing;
Since that all things thou wouldst praise
Beauty took from those who loved them
        In other days.

A Song of Enchantment

A Song of Enchantment I sang me there,
In a green—green wood, by waters fair,
Just as the words came up to me
I sang it under the wild wood tree.

Widdershins turned I, singing it low,
Watching the wild birds come and go;
No cloud in the deep dark blue to be seen
Under the thick-thatched branches green.

Twilight came; silence came;
The planet of evening's silver flame;
By darkening paths I wandered through
Thickets trembling with drops of dew.

But the music is lost and the words are gone
Of the song I sang as I sat alone,
Ages and ages have fallen on me—
On the wood and the pool and the elder tree.

SIR ARTHUR QUILLER-COUCH

1863-1944

Upon Eckington Bridge, River Avon

O pastoral heart of England! like a psalm
  Of green days telling with a quiet beat—
O wave into the sunset flowing calm!
  O tirèd lark descending on the wheat!
Lies it all peace beyond that western fold
  Where now the lingering shepherd sees his star
Rise upon Malvern? Paints an Age of Gold
    Yon cloud with prophecies of linkèd ease—
    Lulling this Land, with hills drawn up like knees,
  To drowse beside her implements of war?

Man shall outlast his battles. They have swept
  Avon from Naseby Field to Severn Ham;
And Evesham's dedicated stones have stepped
  Down to the dust with Montfort's oriflamme.
Nor the red tear nor the reflected tower
  Abides; but yet these eloquent grooves remain,
Worn in the sandstone parapet hour by hour
    By labouring bargemen where they shifted ropes.
    E'en so shall man turn back from violent hopes
  To Adam's cheer, and toil with spade again.

Ay, and his mother Nature, to whose lap
  Like a repentant child at length he hies,
Not in the whirlwind or the thunder-clap
  Proclaims her more tremendous mysteries:
But when in winter's grave, bereft of light,
  With still, small voice divinelier whispering
—Lifting the green head of the aconite,
    Feeding with sap of hope the hazel-shoot—
    She feels God's finger active at the root,
  Turns in her sleep, and murmurs of the Spring.

362

GILBERT KEITH CHESTERTON

1874-1936

The Secret People

Smile at us, pay us, pass us; but do not quite forget,
For we are the people of England, that never have spoken yet.
There is many a fat farmer that drinks less cheerfully,
There is many a free French peasant who is richer and sadder
    than we.
There are no folk in the whole world so helpless or so wise.
There is hunger in our bellies, there is laughter in our eyes;
You laugh at us and love us, both mugs and eyes are wet:
Only you do not know us. For we have not spoken yet.

The fine French kings came over in a flutter of flags and dames.
We liked their smiles and battles, but we never could say their
    names.
The blood ran red to Bosworth and the high French lords
    went down;
There was naught but a naked people under a naked crown.
And the eyes of the King's Servants turned terribly every way,
And the gold of the King's Servants rose higher every day.
They burnt the homes of the shaven men, that had been
    quaint and kind,
Till there was no bed in a monk's house, nor food that man
    could find.
The inns of God where no man paid, that were the wall of the
    weak,
The King's Servants ate them all. And still we did not speak.

And the face of the King's Servants grew greater than the
    King:
He tricked them, and they trapped him, and stood round him
    in a ring.
The new grave lords closed round him, that had eaten the
    abbey's fruits,
And the men of the new religion, with their bibles in their
    boots,

We saw their shoulders moving, to menace or discuss,
And some were pure and some were vile; but none took heed
    of us.
We saw the King as they killed him, and his face was proud
    and pale;
And a few men talked of freedom, while England talked of ale.

A war that we understood not came over the world and woke
Americans, Frenchmen, Irish; but we knew not the things
    they spoke.
They talked about rights and nature and peace and the
    people's reign:
And the squires, our masters, bade us fight; and never
    scorned us again.
Weak if we be for ever, could none condemn us then;
Men called us serfs and drudges; men knew that we were
    men.

In foam and flame at Trafalgar, on Albuera plains,
We did and died like lions, to keep ourselves in chains,
We lay in living ruins; firing and fearing not
The strange fierce face of the Frenchmen who knew for what
    they fought,
And the man who seemed to be more than man we strained
    against and broke;
And we broke our own rights with him. And still we never
    spoke.

Our patch of glory ended; we never heard guns again.
But the squire seemed struck in the saddle; he was foolish, as
    if in pain
He leaned on a staggering lawyer, he clutched a cringing Jew,
He was stricken; it may be, after all, he was stricken at
    Waterloo.
Or perhaps the shades of the shaven men, whose spoil is in his
    house,
Come back in shining shapes at last to spoil his last carouse:
We only know the last sad squires ride slowly towards the sea,
And a new people takes the land: and still it is not we.

They have given us into the hands of the new unhappy lords,
Lords without anger and honour, who dare not carry their
swords.
They fight by shuffling papers; they have bright dead alien
eyes;
They look at our labour and laughter as a tired man looks at
flies.
And the load of their loveless pity is worse than the ancient
wrongs,
Their doors are shut in the evening; and they know no songs.

We hear men speaking for us of new laws strong and sweet,
Yet is there no man speaketh as we speak in the street.
It may be we shall rise the last as Frenchmen rose the first,
Our wrath come after Russia's wrath and our wrath be the
worst.
It may be we are meant to mark with our riot and our rest
God's scorn for all men governing. It may be beer is best.
But we are the people of England; and we have not spoken
yet.
Smile at us, pay us, pass us. But do not quite forget.

The Rolling English Road

Before the Roman came to Rye or out to Severn strode,
The rolling English drunkard made the rolling English road.
A reeling road, a rolling road, that rambles round the shire,
And after him the parson ran, the sexton and the squire;
A merry road, a mazy road, and such as we did tread
The night we went to Birmingham by way of Beachy Head.

I knew no harm of Bonaparte and plenty of the Squire,
And for to fight the Frenchman I did not much desire;
But I did bash their baggonets because they came arrayed
To straighten out the crooked road an English drunkard made,
Where you and I went down the lane with ale-mugs in our
hands,
The night we went to Glastonbury by way of Goodwin Sands.

His sins they were forgiven him; or why do flowers run
Behind him; and the hedges all strengthening in the sun?
The wild thing went from left to right and knew not which
    was which,
But the wild rose was above him when they found him in the
    ditch.
God pardon us, nor harden us; we did not see so clear
The night we went to Bannockburn by way of Brighton Pier.

My friends, we will not go again or ape an ancient rage,
Or stretch the folly of our youth to be the shame of age,
But walk with clearer eyes and ears this path that wandereth,
And see undrugged in evening light the decent inn of death;
For there is good news yet to hear and fine things to be seen,
Before we go to Paradise by way of Kensal Green.

The Praise of Dust

'What of vile dust?' the preacher said.
    Methought the whole world woke,
The dead stone lived beneath my foot,
    And my whole body spoke.

'You, that play tyrant to the dust,
    And stamp its wrinkled face,
This patient star that flings you not
    Far into homeless space,

'Come down out of your dusty shrine
    The living dust to see,
The flowers that at your sermon's end
    Stand blazing silently.

'Rich white and blood-red blossom; stones,
    Lichens like fire encrust;
A gleam of blue, a glare of gold,
    The vision of the dust.

'Pass them all by: till, as you come
  Where, at a city's edge,
Under a tree—I know it well—
  Under a lattice ledge,

'The sunshine falls on one brown head.
  You, too, O cold of clay,
Eater of stones, may haply hear
  The trumpets of that day.

'When God to all His paladins
  By His own splendour swore
To make a fairer face than heaven,
  Of dust and nothing more.'

JOHN MASEFIELD

b. 1878

Beauty

I have seen dawn and sunset on moors and windy hills
Coming in solemn beauty like slow old tunes of Spain:
I have seen the lady April bringing the daffodils,
Bringing the springing grass and the soft warm April rain.

I have heard the song of the blossoms and the old chant of
    the sea,
And seen strange lands from under the arched white sails of
    ships;
But the loveliest things of beauty God ever has showed to me,
Are her voice, and her hair, and eyes, and the dear red curve
    of her lips.

On Eastnor Knoll

Silent are the woods, and the dim green boughs are
Hushed in the twilight: yonder, in the path through
The apple orchard, is a tired plough-boy
Calling the cows home.

A bright white star blinks, the pale moon rounds, but
Still the red, lurid wreckage of the sunset
Smoulders in smoky fire, and burns on
The misty hill-tops.

Ghostly it grows, and darker, the burning
Fades into smoke, and now the gusty oaks are
A silent army of phantoms thronging
A land of shadows.

On Malvern Hill

A wind is brushing down the clover,
   It sweeps the tossing branches bare,
Blowing the poising kestrel over
   The crumbling ramparts of the Caer.

It whirls the scattered leaves before us
   Along the dusty road to home,
Once it awakened into chorus
   The heart-strings in the ranks of Rome.

There by the gusty coppice border
   The shrilling trumpets broke the halt,
The Roman line, the Roman order,
   Swayed forwards to the blind assault.

Spearman and charioteer and bowman
   Charged and were scattered into spray,
Savage and taciturn the Roman
   Hewed upwards in the Roman way.

There—in the twilight—where the cattle
   Are lowing home across the fields,
The beaten warriors left the battle
   Dead on the clansmen's wicker shields.

The leaves whirl in the wind's riot
  Beneath the Beacon's jutting spur,
Quiet are clan and chief, and quiet
  Centurion and signifer.

The West Wind

It's a warm wind, the west wind, full of birds' cries;
I never hear the west wind but tears are in my eyes.
For it comes from the west lands, the old brown hills,
And April's in the west wind, and daffodils.

It's a fine land, the west land, for hearts as tired as mine,
Apple orchards blossom there, and the air's like wine.
There is cool green grass there, where men may lie at rest,
And the thrushes are in song there, fluting from the nest.

'Will ye not come home, brother? Ye have been long away.
It's April, and blossom time, and white is the may;
And bright is the sun, brother, and warm is the rain,—
Will ye not come home, brother, home to us again?

'The young corn is green, brother, where the rabbits run,
It's blue sky, and white clouds, and warm rain and sun.
It's song to a man's soul, brother, fire to a man's brain,
To hear the wild bees and see the merry spring again.

'Larks are singing in the west, brother, above the green wheat,
So will ye not come home, brother, and rest your tired feet?
I've a balm for bruised hearts, brother, sleep for aching eyes,'
Says the warm wind, the west wind, full of birds' cries.

It's the white road westwards is the road I must tread
To the green grass, the cool grass, and rest for heart and head,
To the violets and the warm hearts and the thrushes' song,
In the fine land, the west land, the land where I belong.

The Seekers

Friends and loves we have none, nor wealth nor blest abode,
But the hope of the City of God at the other end of the road.

Not for us are content, and quiet, and peace of mind,
For we go seeking a city that we shall never find.

There is no solace on earth for us—for such as we—
Who search for a hidden city that we shall never see.

Only the road and the dawn, the sun, the wind, and the rain,
And the watch fire under stars, and sleep, and the road again.

We seek the City of God, and the haunt where beauty dwells,
And we find the noisy mart and the sound of burial bells.

Never the golden city, where radiant people meet,
But the dolorous town where mourners are going about the
street.

We travel the dusty road till the light of the day is dim,
And sunset shows us spires away on the world's rim.

We travel from dawn to dusk, till the day is past and by,
Seeking the Holy City beyond the rim of the sky.

Friends and loves we have none, nor wealth nor blest abode,
But the hope of the City of God at the other end of the road.

EDWARD THOMAS

1878-1917

If I should ever by Chance

If I should ever by chance grow rich
I'll buy Codham, Cockridden, and Childerditch,
Roses, Pyrgo, and Lapwater,
And let them all to my elder daughter.
The rent I shall ask of her will be only
Each year's first violets, white and lonely,

The first primroses and orchises—
She must find them before I do, that is.
But if she finds a blossom on furze
Without rent they shall all for ever be hers,
Codham, Cockridden, and Childerditch,
Roses, Pyrgo, and Lapwater,—
I shall give them all to my elder daughter.

WILFRID WILSON GIBSON

b. 1878

The Blue-peter

The day has come for sailing; and at last
The brisk blue-peter flutters at the mast.
Too long beneath the mountains we have lain
While winds and waters called to us in vain:
Too long the inn has held us, and too long
Our ears have hearkened to the tavern-song.
The time has come to quit the company
Of those who dread the isolating sea,
Who, slumbering through night-watches, spend their days
Carousing in the ingle's drowsy blaze:
For what are they to us who are the sons
Of tempest, in whose veins the salt tide runs,
Whose pulses answer to the ebb and flow
Of all the seas that travel to and fro,
Whose feet have trod the tilting deck from birth
And stumble only on the stable earth,
Whose eyes can pierce the spindrift of the night
And blunder blindfold in the tavern light,
Whose hearts must ever in the throng and press
Ache with intolerable loneliness
Shut in by walls as in an airless grave,
Whose home is the unwalled unraftered wave,
Who each within himself can only find
In solitude the comrade to his mind,
And only in the lone sea-watch can be
At ease at length in his own company.

The brisk blue-peter beckons; and at last
Our souls shall ride full-sailed before the blast
Into the perilous security
Of strife with the uncompromising sea.

The Ice-cart

Perched on my city office stool
I watched with envy, while a cool
And lucky carter handled ice . . .
And I was wandering in a trice,
Far from the gray and grimy heat
Of that intolerable street
O'er sapphire berg and emerald floe
Beneath the still cold ruby glow
Of everlasting Polar night,
Bewildered by the queer half-light,
Until I stumbled unawares
Upon a creek where big white bears
Plunged headlong down with flourished heels
And floundered after shining seals
Through shivering seas of blinding blue.
And, as I watched them, ere I knew
I'd stripped and I was swimming too
Among the seal-pack, young and hale,
And thrusting on with threshing tail,
With twist and twirl and sudden leap
Through crackling ice and salty deep,
Diving and doubling with my kind
Until at last we left behind
Those big white, blundering bulks of death
And lay, at length, with panting breath
Upon a far untravelled floe
Beneath a gentle drift of snow—
Snow drifting gently fine and white
Out of the endless Polar night,
Falling and falling evermore
Upon that far untravelled shore

Till I was buried fathoms deep
Beneath that cold, white drifting sleep—
Sleep drifting deep,
Deep drifting sleep. . . .

The carter cracked a sudden whip:
I clutched my stool with startled grip,
Awakening to the grimy heat
Of that intolerable street.

HAROLD MONRO

1879-1932

Solitude

When you have tidied all things for the night,
And while your thoughts are fading to their sleep,
You'll pause a moment in the late firelight,
Too sorrowful to weep.

The large and gentle furniture has stood
In sympathetic silence all the day
With that old kindness of domestic wood;
Nevertheless the haunted room will say:
'Some one must be away.'

The little dog rolls over half awake,
Stretches his paws, yawns, looking up at you,
Wags his tail very slightly for your sake,
That you may feel he is unhappy too.

A distant engine whistles, or the floor
Creaks, or the wandering night-wind bangs a door.

Silence is scattered like a broken glass.
The minutes prick their ears and run about,
Then one by one subside again and pass
Sedately in, monotonously out.

You bend your head and wipe away a tear.
Solitude walks one heavy step more near.

JAMES STEPHENS

1882-1950

The Shell

I

And then I pressed the shell
Close to my ear,
And listened well.

And straightway, like a bell,
Came low and clear
The slow, sad, murmur of far distant seas

Whipped by an icy breeze
Upon a shore
Wind-swept and desolate.

It was a sunless strand that never bore
The footprint of a man,
Nor felt the weight

Since time began
Of any human quality or stir,
Save what the dreary winds and waves incur.

II

And in the hush of waters was the sound
Of pebbles, rolling round;
For ever rolling, with a hollow sound:

And bubbling sea-weeds, as the waters go,
Swish to and fro
Their long, cold tentacles of slimy grey:

There was no day;
Nor ever came a night
Setting the stars alight

To wonder at the moon:
Was twilight only, and the frightened croon,
Smitten to whimpers, of the dreary wind

And waves that journeyed blind . . .
And then I loosed my ear—Oh, it was sweet
To hear a cart go jolting down the street.

In the Poppy Field

Mad Patsy said, he said to me,
That every morning he could see
An angel walking on the sky;
Across the sunny skies of morn
He threw great handfuls far and nigh
Of poppy seed among the corn;
—And then, he said, the angels run
To see the poppies in the sun—

—A poppy is a devil weed,—
I said to him—he disagreed:
He said the devil had no hand
In spreading flowers tall and fair
By corn and rye and meadow land,
And gurth and barrow everywhere:
The devil has not any flower,
But only money in his power.

And then he stretched out in the sun,
And rolled upon his back for fun!
He kicked his legs and roared for joy
Because the sun was shining down!
He said he was a little boy
And wouldn't work for any clown!
He ran and laughed behind a bee;
And danced for very ecstasy!

The Fifteen Acres

I

I cling and swing
On a branch, or sing
Through the cool clear hush of morning O!

Or fling my wing
On the air, and bring
To sleepier birds a warning O!

That the night's in flight!
And the sun's in sight!
And the dew is the grass adorning O!

And the green leaves swing
As I sing, sing, sing:
Up by the river,
Down by the dell,
To the little wee nest,
Where the big tree fell,
So early in the morning O!

II

I flit and twit
In the sun for a bit,
When his light so bright is shining O!

Or sit, and fit
My plumes, or knit
Straw plaits for the nest's nice lining O!

And she, with glee,
Shows unto me,
Underneath her wings reclining O!

And I sing that Peg,
Has an egg, egg, egg!
    Up by the oat-field,
     Round the mill;
    Past the meadow,
     Down the hill;
    So early in the morning O!

III

I stoop and swoop
  On the air, or loop
Through the trees, and then go soaring O!

To group, with a troop
  On the skiey poop,
While the wind behind is roaring O!

I skim and swim
  By a cloud's red rim;
And up to the azure flooring O!

And my wide wings drip,
  As I slip, slip, slip,
    Down through the rain-drops,
     Back where Peg
    Broods in the nest
     On the little white egg,
    So early in the morning O!

The Goat Paths

I

The crooked paths
Go every way
Upon the hill
—They wind about
Through the heather,

In and out
Of a quiet
Sunniness.

And the goats,
Day after day,
Stray
In sunny
Quietness;
Cropping here,
And cropping there
—As they pause,
And turn,
And pass—
Now a bit
Of heather spray,
Now a mouthful
Of the grass.

II

In the deeper
Sunniness;
In the place
Where nothing stirs;
Quietly
In quietness;
In the quiet
Of the furze
They stand a while;
They dream;
They lie;
They stare
Upon the roving sky.

If you approach
They run away!
They will stare,
And stamp,
And bound,

With a sudden angry sound,
To the sunny
Quietude;
To crouch again,
Where nothing stirs,
In the quiet
Of the furze:
To crouch them down again,
And brood,
In the sunny
Solitude.

III

Were I but
As free
As they,
I would stray
Away
And brood;
I would beat
A hidden way,
Through the quiet
Heather spray,
To a sunny
Solitude.

And should you come
I'd run away!
I would make an angry sound,
I would stare,
And stamp,
And bound
To the deeper
Quietude;
To the place
Where nothing stirs
In the quiet
Of the furze.

IV

In that airy
Quietness
I would dream
As long as they:
Through the quiet
Sunniness
I would stray
Away
And brood,
All among
The heather spray,
In a sunny
Solitude.

—I would think
Until I found
Something
I can never find;
—Something
Lying
On the ground,
In the bottom
Of my mind.

JOHN DRINKWATER

1882-1937

Moonlit Apples

At the top of the house the apples are laid in rows,
And the skylight lets the moonlight in, and those
Apples are deep-sea apples of green.   There goes
    A cloud on the moon in the autumn night.

A mouse in the wainscot scratches, and scratches, and then
There is no sound at the top of the house of men
Or mice; and the cloud is blown, and the moon again
    Dapples the apples with deep-sea light.

They are lying in rows there, under the gloomy beams;
On the sagging floor; they gather the silver streams
Out of the moon, those moonlit apples of dreams,
    And quiet is the steep stair under.

In the corridors under there is nothing but sleep.
And stiller than ever on orchard boughs they keep
Tryst with the moon, and deep is the silence, deep
    On moon-washed apples of wonder.

JAMES ELROY FLECKER

1884-1915

The Golden Journey to Samarkand

PROLOGUE

We who with songs beguile your pilgrimage
    And swear that Beauty lives though lilies die,
We Poets of the proud old lineage
    Who sing to find your hearts, we know not why,—

What shall we tell you? Tales, marvellous tales
    Of ships and stars and isles where good men rest,
Where nevermore the rose of sunset pales,
    And winds and shadows fall toward the West:

And there the world's first huge white-bearded kings
    In dim glades sleeping, murmur in their sleep,
And closer round their breasts the ivy clings,
    Cutting its pathway slow and red and deep.

II

And how beguile you? Death has no repose
    Warmer and deeper than that Orient sand
Which hides the beauty and bright faith of those
    Who made the Golden Journey to Samarkand.

And now they wait and whiten peaceably,
　　Those conquerors, those poets, those so fair:
They know time comes, not only you and I,
　　But the whole world shall whiten, here or there;

When those long caravans that cross the plain
　　With dauntless feet and sound of silver bells
Put forth no more for glory or for gain,
　　Take no more solace from the palm-girt wells.

When the great markets by the sea shut fast
　　All that calm Sunday that goes on and on:
When even lovers find their peace at last,
　　And Earth is but a star, that once had shone.

The Old Ships

I have seen old ships sail like swans asleep
Beyond the village which men still call Tyre,
With leaden age o'ercargoed, dipping deep
For Famagusta and the hidden sun
That rings black Cyprus with a lake of fire;
And all those ships were certainly so old—
Who knows how oft with squat and noisy gun,
Questing brown slaves or Syrian oranges,
The pirate Genoese
Hell-raked them till they rolled
Blood, water, fruit and corpses up the hold.
But now through friendly seas they softly run,
Painted the mid-sea blue or shore-sea green,
Still patterned with the vine and grapes in gold.

But I have seen
Pointing her shapely shadows from the dawn
An image tumbled on a rose-swept bay,
A drowsy ship of some yet older day;
And, wonder's breath indrawn,

Thought I—who knows—who knows— but in that same
(Fished up beyond Aeaea, patched up new
—Stern painted brighter blue—)
That talkative, bald-headed seaman came
(Twelve patient comrades sweating at the oar)
From Troy's doom-crimson shore,
And with great lies about his wooden horse
Set the crew laughing, and forgot his course.
It was so old a ship—who knows—who knows?
—And yet so beautiful, I watched in vain
To see the mast burst open with a rose,
And the whole deck put on its leaves again.

DAVID HERBERT LAWRENCE

1885-1930

Snake

A snake came to my water-trough
On a hot, hot day, and I in pyjamas for the heat,
To drink there.

In the deep, strange-scented shade of the great dark carob-tree
I came down the steps with my pitcher
And must wait, must stand and wait, for there he was at the
    trough before me.

He reached down from a fissure in the earth-wall in the gloom
And trailed his yellow-brown slackness soft-bellied down, over
    the edge of the stone trough
And rested his throat upon the stone bottom,
And where the water had dripped from the tap, in a small
    clearness,
He sipped with his straight mouth,
Softly drank through his straight gums, into his slack long
    body,
Silently.

N

Someone was before me at my water-trough,
And I, like a second comer, waiting.

He lifted his head from his drinking, as cattle do,
And looked at me vaguely, as drinking cattle do,
And flickered his two-forked tongue from his lips, and mused
    a moment,
And stooped and drank a little more,
Being earth-brown, earth-golden from the burning bowels of
    the earth
On the day of Sicilian July, with Etna smoking.

The voice of my education said to me
He must be killed,
For in Sicily the black, black snakes are innocent, the gold
    are venomous.

And voices in me said, If you were a man
You would take a stick and break him now, and finish him
    off.

But must I confess how I liked him,
How glad I was he had come like a guest in quiet, to drink
    at my water-trough
And depart peaceful, pacified, and thankless,
Into the burning bowels of this earth?

Was it cowardice, that I dared not kill him?
Was it perversity, that I longed to talk to him?
Was it humility, to feel so honoured?
I felt so honoured.

And yet those voices:
If you were not afraid, you would kill him!

And truly I was afraid, I was most afraid,
But even so, honoured still more
That he should seek my hospitality
From out the dark door of the secret earth.

He drank enough
And lifted his head, dreamily, as one who has drunken,
And flickered his tongue like a forked night on the air, so
    black,
Seeming to lick his lips,
And looked around like a god, unseeing, into the air,
And slowly turned his head,
And slowly, very slowly, as if thrice adream,
Proceeded to draw his slow length curving round
And climb again the broken bank of my wall-face.

And as he put his head into that dreadful hole,
And as he slowly drew up, snake-easing his shoulders, and
    entered farther,
A sort of horror, a sort of protest against his withdrawing into
    that horrid black hole,
Deliberately going into the blackness, and slowly drawing
    himself after,
Overcame me now his back was turned.

I looked round, I put down my pitcher,
I picked up a clumsy log
And threw it at the water-trough with a clatter.

I think it did not hit him,
But suddenly that part of him that was left behind convulsed
    in undignified haste,
Writhed like lightning, and was gone
Into the black hole, the earth-lipped fissure in the wall-front,
At which, in the intense still noon, I stared with fascination.

And immediately I regretted it.
I thought how paltry, how vulgar, what a mean act!
I despised myself and the voices of my accursed human
    education.

And I thought of the albatross,
And I wished he would come back, my snake.

For he seemed to me again like a king,
Like a king in exile, uncrowned in the underworld,
Now due to be crowned again.

And so, I missed my chance with one of the lords
Of life.
And I have something to expiate;
A pettiness.

SIEGFRIED SASSOON

b. 1886

Morning Express

Along the wind-swept platform, pinched and white,
The travellers stand in pools of wintry light,
Offering themselves to morn's long, slanting arrows.
The train's due; porters trundle laden barrows.
The train steams in, volleying resplendent clouds
Of sun-blown vapour. Hither and about,
Scared people hurry, storming the doors in crowds.
The officials seem to waken with a shout,
Resolved to hoist and plunder; some to the vans
Leap; others rumble the milk in gleaming cans.

Boys, indolent-eyed, from baskets leaning back,
Question each face; a man with a hammer steals
Stooping from coach to coach; with clang and clack,
Touches and tests, and listens to the wheels.

Guard sounds a warning whistle, points to the clock
With brandished flag, and on his folded flock
Claps the last door: the monster grunts: 'Enough!'
Tightening his load of links with pant and puff.
Under the arch, then forth into blue day,
Glide the processional windows on their way,
And glimpse the stately folk who sit at ease
To view the world like kings taking the seas
In prosperous weather: drifting banners tell
Their progress to the counties; with them goes
The clamour of their journeying; while those
Who sped them stand to wave a last farewell.

Everyone Sang

Everyone suddenly burst out singing;
And I was filled with such delight
As prisoned birds must find in freedom
Winging wildly across the white
Orchards and dark green fields; on; on; and out of sight.

Everyone's voice was suddenly lifted,
And beauty came like the setting sun.
My heart was shaken with tears, and horror
Drifted away. . . . O, but every one
Was a bird; and the song was wordless; the singing will
    never be done.

RUPERT BROOKE

1887-1915

The Fish

In a cool curving world he lies
And ripples with dark ecstasies.
The kind luxurious lapse and steal
Shapes all his universe to feel

And know and be; the clinging stream
Closes his memory, glooms his dream,
Who lips the roots o' the shore, and glides
Superb on unreturning tides.
Those silent waters weave for him
A fluctuant mutable world and dim,
Where wavering masses bulge and gape
Mysterious, and shape to shape
Dies momently through whorl and hollow,
And form and line and solid follow
Solid and line and form to dream
Fantastic down the eternal stream;
An obscure world, a shifting world,
Bulbous, or pulled to thin, or curled,
Or serpentine, or driving arrows,
Or serene slidings, or March narrows.
There slipping wave and shore are one,
And weed and mud. No ray of sun,
But glow to glow fades down the deep
(As dream to unknown dream in sleep);
Shaken translucency illumes
The hyaline of drifting glooms;
The strange soft-handed depth subdues
Drowned colour there, but black to hues,
As death to living, decomposes—
Red darkness of the heart of roses,
Blue brilliant from dead starless skies,
And gold that lies behind the eyes,
The unknown unnameable sightless white
That is the essential flame of night,
Lustreless purple, hooded green,
The myriad hues that lie between
Darkness and darkness! . . .

                                And all's one,
Gentle, embracing, quiet, dun,
The world he rests in, world he knows,
Perpetual curving. Only—grows

An eddy in that ordered falling,
A knowledge from the gloom, a calling
Weed in the wave, gleam in the mud—
The dark fire leaps along his blood;
Dateless and deathless, blind and still,
The intricate impulse works its will;
His woven world drops back; and he,
Sans providence, sans memory,
Unconscious and directly driven,
Fades to some dank sufficient heaven.

O world of lips, O world of laughter,
Where hope is fleet and thought flies after,
Of lights in the clear night, of cries
That drift along the wave and rise
Thin to the glittering stars above,
You know the hands, the eyes of love!
The strife of limbs, the sightless clinging,
The infinitive distance, and the singing
Blown by the wind, a flame of sound,
The gleam, the flowers, and vast around
The horizon, and the heights above—
You know the sigh, the song of love!

But there the night is close, and there
Darkness is cold and strange and bare;
And the secret deeps are whisperless;
And rhythm is all deliciousness;
And joy is in the throbbing tide,
Whose intricate fingers beat and glide
In felt bewildering harmonies
Of trembling touch; and music is
The exquisite knocking of the blood.
Space is no more, under the mud;
His bliss is older than the sun.
Silent and straight the waters run.
The lights, the cries, the willows dim,
And the dark tide are one with him.

The Soldier

If I should die, think only this of me:
    That there's some corner of a foreign field
That is for ever England.   There shall be
    In that rich earth a richer dust concealed;
A dust whom England bore, shaped, made aware,
    Gave, once, her flowers to love, her ways to roam,
A body of England's, breathing English air,
    Washed by the rivers, blest by suns of home.
And think, this heart, all evil shed away,
    A pulse in the eternal mind, no less
        Gives somewhere back the thoughts by England given;
Her sights and sounds; dreams happy as her day;
    And laughter, learnt of friends; and gentleness,
        In hearts at peace, under an English heaven.

The Great Lover

I have been so great a lover; filled my days
So proudly with the splendour of Love's praise,
The pain, the calm, and the astonishment,
Desire illimitable, and still content,
And all dear names men use, to cheat despair,
For the perplexed and viewless streams that bear
Our hearts at random down the dark of life.
Now, ere the unthinking silence on that strife
Steals down, I would cheat drowsy Death so far,
My night shall be remembered for a star
That outshone all the suns of all men's days.
Shall I not crown them with immortal praise
Whom I have loved, who have given me, dared with me
High secrets, and in darkness knelt to see
The inenarrable godhead of delight?
Love is a flame;—we have beaconed the world's night.
A city:—and we have built it, these and I.
An emperor:—we have taught the world to die.
So, for their sakes I loved, ere I go hence,
And the high cause of Love's magnificence,

And to keep loyalties young, I'll write those names
Golden for ever, eagles, crying flames,
And set them as a banner, that men may know,
To dare the generations, burn, and blow
Out on the wind of Time, shining and streaming. . . .

These I have loved:
                    White plates and cups, clean-gleaming,
Ringed with blue lines; and feathery, faery dust;
Wet roofs, beneath the lamp-light; the strong crust
Of friendly bread; and many-tasting food;
Rainbows; and the blue bitter smoke of wood;
And radiant raindrops couching in cool flowers;
And flowers themselves, that sway through sunny hours,
Dreaming of moths that drink them under the moon;
Then, the cool kindliness of sheets, that soon
Smooth away trouble; and the rough male kiss
Of blankets; grainy wood; live hair that is
Shining and free; blue-massing clouds; the keen
Unpassioned beauty of a great machine;
The benison of hot water; furs to touch;
The good smell of old clothes; and other such—
The comfortable smell of friendly fingers,
Hair's fragrance, and the musty reek that lingers
About dead leaves and last year's ferns. . . .
                                        Dear names,
And thousand other throng to me! Royal flames;
Sweet water's dimpling laugh from tap or spring;
Holes in the ground; and voices that do sing;
Voices in laughter, too; and body's pain,
Soon turned to peace; and the deep-panting train;
Firm sands; the little dulling edge of foam
That browns and dwindles as the wave goes home;
And washen stones, gay for an hour; the cold
Graveness of iron; moist black earthen mould;
Sleep; and high places; footprints in the dew;
And oaks; and brown horse-chestnuts, glossy-new;
And new-peeled sticks; and shining pools on grass;—
All these have been my loves. And these shall pass,

N*

Whatever passes not, in the great hour,
Nor all my passion, all my prayers, have power
To hold them with me through the gate of Death.
They'll play deserter, turn with the traitor breath,
Break the high bond we made, and sell Love's trust
And sacramented covenant to the dust.
—Oh, never a doubt but, somewhere, I shall wake,
And give what's left of love again, and make
New friends, now strangers. . . .
                  But the best I've known
Stays here, and changes, breaks, grows old, is blown
About the winds of the world, and fades from brains
Of living men, and dies.
                Nothing remains.

O dear my loves, O faithless, once again
This one last gift I give: that after men
Shall know, and later lovers, far-removed,
Praise you 'All these were lovely'; say, 'He loved.'

The Old Vicarage, Grantchester

Café des Westens, Berlin, May 1912

Just now the lilac is in bloom,
All before my little room;
And in my flower-beds, I think,
Smile the carnation and the pink;
And down the borders, well I know,
The poppy and the pansy blow. . . .
Oh! there the chestnuts, summer through,
Beside the river make for you
A tunnel of green gloom, and sleep
Deeply above; and green and deep
The stream mysterious glides beneath,
Green as a dream and deep as death.—
Oh, damn! I know it! and I know
How the May fields all golden show,

And when the day is young and sweet,
Gild gloriously the bare feet
That run to bathe. . . .
                Du lieber Gott!

Here am I, sweating, sick, and hot,
And there the shadowed waters fresh
Lean up to embrace the naked flesh.
Temperamentvoll German Jews
Drink beer around; and *there* the dews
Are soft beneath a morn of gold.
Here tulips bloom as they are told;
Unkempt about those hedges blows
An English unofficial rose;
And there the unregulated sun
Slopes down to rest when day is done,
And wakes a vague unpunctual star,
A slippered Hesper; and there are
Meads towards Haslingfield and Coton
Where *das Betreten's* not *verboten* . . .
εἴθε γενοίμην . . . would I were
In Grantchester, in Grantchester!—
Some, it may be, can get in touch
With Nature there, or Earth, or such.
And clever modern men have seen
A Faun a-peeping through the green,
And felt the Classics were not dead,
To glimpse a Naiad's reedy head,
Or hear the Goat-foot piping low. . . .
But these are things I do not know.
I only know that you may lie
Day long and watch the Cambridge sky,
And, flower-lulled in sleepy grass,
Hear the cool lapse of hours pass,
Until the centuries blend and blur
In Grantchester, in Grantchester. . . .
Still in the dawnlit waters cool
His ghostly Lordship swims his pool,
And tries the strokes, essays the tricks,
Long learnt on Hellespont, or Styx;

Dan Chaucer hears his river still
Chatter beneath a phantom mill.
Tennyson notes, with studious eye,
How Cambridge waters hurry by. . . .
And in that garden, black and white,
Creep whispers through the grass all night;
And spectral dance, before the dawn,
A hundred Vicars down the lawn;
Curates, long dust, will come and go
On lissom, clerical, printless toe;
And oft between the boughs is seen
The sly shade of a Rural Dean. . . .
Till, at a shiver in the skies,
Vanishing with Satanic cries,
The prim ecclesiastic rout
Leaves but a startled sleeper-out,
Grey heavens, the first bird's drowsy calls,
The falling house that never falls.

God! I will pack, and take a train,
And get me to England once again!
For England's the one land, I know,
Where men with Splendid Hearts may go;
And Cambridgeshire, of all England,
The shire for Men who Understand;
And of *that* district I prefer
The lovely hamlet Grantchester.
For Cambridge people rarely smile,
Being urban, squat, and packed with guile;
And Royston men in the far South
Are black and fierce and strange of mouth;
At Over they fling oaths at one,
And worse than oaths at Trumpington,
And Ditton girls are mean and dirty,
And there's none in Harston under thirty,
And folks in Shelford and those parts,
Have twisted lips and twisted hearts,
And Barton men make cockney rhymes,
And Coton's full of nameless crimes,

And things are done you'd not believe
At Madingley on Christmas Eve.
Strong men have run for miles and miles
When one from Cherry Hinton smiles;
Strong men have blanched, and shot their wives,
Rather than send them to St. Ives;
Strong men have cried like babes, bydam,
To hear what happened at Babraham.
But Grantchester! ah, Grantchester!
There's peace and holy quiet there,
Great clouds along pacific skies,
And men and women with straight eyes,
Lithe children lovelier than a dream,
A bosky wood, a slumbrous stream,
And little kindly winds that creep
Round twilight corners, half asleep.
In Grantchester their skins are white,
They bathe by day, they bathe by night;
The women there do all they ought;
The men observe the Rules of Thought.
They love the Good; they worship Truth;
They laugh uproariously in youth;
(And when they get to feeling old,
They up and shoot themselves, I'm told). . . .

Ah God! to see the branches stir
Across the moon at Grantchester!
To smell the thrilling-sweet and rotten,
Unforgettable, unforgotten
River-smell, and hear the breeze
Sobbing in the little trees.
Say, do the elm-clumps greatly stand,
Still guardians of that holy land?
The chestnuts shade, in reverend dream,
The yet unacademic stream?
Is dawn a secret shy and cold
Anadyomene, silver-gold?
And sunset still a golden sea
From Haslingfield to Madingley?

And after, ere the night is born,
Do hares come out about the corn?
Oh, is the water sweet and cool,
Gentle and brown, above the pool?
And laughs the immortal river still
Under the mill, under the mill?
Say, is there Beauty yet to find?
And Certainty? and Quiet kind?
Deep meadows yet, for to forget
The lies, and truths, and pain? . . . oh! yet
Stands the Church clock at ten to three?
And is there honey still for tea?

JULIAN GRENFELL

1888-1915

Into Battle

The naked earth is warm with spring,
　And with green grass and bursting trees
Leans to the sun's gaze glorying,
　And quivers in the sunny breeze;
And Life is colour and warmth and light,
　And a striving evermore for these;
And he is dead who will not fight;
　And who dies fighting has increase.

The fighting man shall from the sun
　Take warmth, and life from the glowing earth;
Speed with the light-foot winds to run,
　And with the trees to newer birth;
And find, when fighting shall be done,
　Great rest, and fullness after dearth.

All the bright company of Heaven
　Hold him in their high comradeship,
The Dog-Star and the Sisters Seven,
　Orion's Belt and sworded hip.

The woodland trees that stand together,
  They stand to him each one a friend;
They gently speak in the windy weather;
  They guide to valley and ridge's end.

The kestrel hovering by day,
  And the little owls that call by night,
Bid him be swift and keen as they,
  As keen of ear, as swift of sight.

The blackbird sings to him, 'Brother, brother,
  If this be the last song you shall sing,
Sing well, for you may not sing another;
  Brother, sing.'

In dreary, doubtful, waiting hours,
  Before the brazen frenzy starts,
The horses show him nobler powers;
  O patient eyes, courageous hearts!

And when the burning moment breaks,
  And all things else are out of mind,
And only joy of battle takes
  Him by the throat, and makes him blind,

Through joy and blindness he shall know,
  Not caring much to know, that still
Nor lead nor steel shall reach him, so
  That it be not the Destin'd Will.

The thundering line of battle stands,
  And in the air Death moans and sings;
But Day shall clasp him with strong hands,
  And Night shall fold him in soft wings.

THOMAS STEARNS ELIOT

b. 1888

The Hollow Men

Mistah Kurtz—he dead

A Penny for the old Guy

I

We are the hollow men
We are the stuffed men
Leaning together
Headpiece filled with straw.   Alas!
Our dried voices, when
We whisper together
Are quiet and meaningless
As wind in dry grass
Or rats' feet over broken glass
In our dry cellar.

Shape without form, shade without colour,
Paralysed force, gesture without motion;

Those who have crossed
With direct eyes to death's other kingdom
Remember us—if at all—not as lost
Violent souls, but only
As the hollow men
The stuffed men.

II

Eyes I dare not meet in dreams
In death's dream kingdom
These do not appear:
There, the eyes are
Sunlight on a broken column
There, is a tree swinging
And voices are
In the wind's singing
More distant and more solemn
Than a fading star.

Let me be no nearer
In death's dream kingdom
Let me also wear
Such deliberate disguises—
Rat's coat, crowskin, crossed staves
In a field
Behaving as the wind behaves
No nearer—

Not that final meeting
In the twilight kingdom.

III

This is the dead land
This is cactus land
Here the stone images
Are raised, here they receive
The supplication of a dead man's hand
Under the twinkle of a fading star.

Is it like this
In death's other kingdom?
Waking alone
At the hour when we are
Trembling with tenderness,
Lips that would kiss
Form prayers to broken stone.

IV

The eyes are not here
There are no eyes here
In this valley of dying stars,
In this hollow valley
This broken jaw of our lost kingdoms
In this last of meeting places
We grope together
And avoid speech
Gathered on this beach of the tumid river

Sightless, unless
The eyes reappear
As the perpetual star
And multifoliate rose
Of death's twilight kingdom
The hope only
Of empty men.

v

Here we go round the prickly pear
Prickly pear prickly pear
Here we go round the prickly pear
At five o'clock in the morning.

Between the idea
And the reality
Between the motion
And the act
Falls the Shadow

For Thine is the Kingdom

Between the conception
And the creation
Between the emotion
And the response
Falls the Shadow

Life is very long

Between the desire
And the spasm
Between the potency
And the existence
Between the essence
And the descent
Falls the Shadow

For Thine is the Kingdom

For thine is
Life is
For Thine is the

This is the way the world ends
This is the way the world ends
This is the way the world ends
Not with a bang but a whimper.

Journey of the Magi

'A cold coming we had of it,
Just the worst time of the year
For a journey, and such a long journey:
The ways deep, and the weather sharp,
The very dead of winter.'
And the camels galled, sore-footed, refractory,
Lying down in the melting snow.
There were times we regretted
The summer palaces on slopes, the terraces,
And the silken girls bringing sherbet.
Then the camel men cursing and grumbling
And running away, and wanting their liquor and women,
And the night-fires going out, and the lack of shelters,
And the cities hostile and the towns unfriendly
And the villages dirty and charging high prices:
A hard time we had of it.
At the end we preferred to travel all night,
Sleeping in snatches,
With the voices singing in our ears, saying
That this was all folly.

Then at dawn we came down to a temperate valley,
Wet, below the snow-line, smelling of vegetation;
With a running stream and a water-mill beating the darkness,
And three trees on the low sky,
And an old white horse galloped away in the meadow.

Then we came to a tavern with vine-leaves over the lintel,
Six hands at an open door dicing for pieces of silver,
And feet kicking the empty wine-skins.
But there was no information, and so we continued
And arrived at evening, not a moment too soon
Finding the place; it was (you may say) satisfactory.

All this was a long time ago, I remember,
And I would do it again, but set down
This set down
This: were we led all that way for
Birth or Death? There was a Birth, certainly,
We had evidence and no doubt. I had seen birth and death,
But had thought they were different; this Birth was
Hard and bitter agony for us, like Death, our death.
We returned to our places, these Kingdoms,
But no longer at ease here, in the old dispensation,
With an alien people clutching their gods.
I should be glad of another death.

EDWIN MUIR

b. 1889

The Road

There **is a** road that turning always
  Cuts off the country of Again.
Archers stand there on every side
  And as it runs Time's deer is slain,
  And lies where it has lain.

That busy clock shows never an hour.
  All flies and all in flight must tarry.
The hunter shoots the empty air
  Far on before the quarry,
  Which falls though nothing's there to parry.

The lion couching in the centre
　　With mountain head and sunset brow
Rolls down the everlasting slope
　　Bones picked an age ago,
　　And the bones rise up and go.

There the beginning finds the end
　　Before beginning ever can be,
And the great runner never leaves
　　The starting and the finishing tree,
　　The budding and the fading tree.

There the ship sailing safe in harbour
　　Long since in many a sea was drowned.
The treasure burning in her hold
　　So near will never be found,
　　Sunk past all sound.

There a man on a summer evening
　　Reclines at ease upon his tomb
And is his mortal effigy.
　　And there within the womb,
　　The cell of doom,

The ancestral deed is thought and done,
　　And in a million Edens fall
A million Adams drowned in darkness,
　　For small is great and great is small,
　　And a blind seed all.

EDWARD SHANKS

1892-1953

The Swimmers

The cove's a shining plate of blue and green,
With darker belts between
The trough and crest of the slow-rising swell,
And the great rocks throw purple shadows down,
Where transient sun-sparks wink and burst and drown
And glimmering pebbles lie too deep to tell,

Hidden or shining as the shadow wavers.
And everywhere the restless sun-steeped air
Trembles and quavers,
As though it were
More saturate with light than it could bear.

Now come the swimmers from slow-dripping caves,
Where the shy fern creeps under the veined roof,
And wading out meet with glad breast the waves.
One holds aloof,
Climbing alone the reef with shrinking feet,
That scarce endure the jagged stones' dull beat
Till on the edge he poises
And flies to cleave the water, vanishing
In wreaths of white, with echoing liquid noises,
And swims beneath, a vague, distorted thing.
Now all the other swimmers leave behind
The crystal shallow and the foam-wet shore,
And sliding into deeper water find
A living coolness in the lifting flood,
And through their bodies leaps the sparkling blood,
So that they feel the faint earth's drought no more.
There now they float, heads raised above the green,
White bodies cloudily seen,
Farther and farther from the brazen rock,
On which the hot air shakes, on which the tide
Fruitlessly throws with gentle, soundless shock
The cool and lagging wave.   Out, out they go,
And now upon a mirrored cloud they ride
Or turning over, with soft strokes and slow,
Slide on like shadows in a tranquil sky.
Behind them, on the tall, parched cliff, the dry
And dusty grasses grow
In shallow ledges of the arid stone,
Starving for coolness and the touch of rain.
But, though to earth they must return again,
Here come the soft sea-airs to meet them, blown
Over the surface of the outer deep,
Scarce moving, staying, falling, straying, gone,
Light and delightful as the touch of sleep. . . .

One wakes and splashes round,
And, as by magic, all the others wake
From that sea-dream, and now with rippling sound
Their rapid arms the enchanted silence break.
And now again the crystal shallows take
The gleaming bodies whose cool hour is done;
They pause upon the beach, they pause and sigh,
Then vanish in the caverns one by one.

Soon the wet foot-marks on the stones are dry:
The cove sleeps on beneath the unwavering sun.

OSBERT SITWELL

b. 1892

Mrs. Hague

Old Mrs. Hague,
The Gardener's wife,
Was not to be enclosed in any formulas.
She seems to stand upon a little mound
Of pansies,
                Primroses,
                                And primulas.
Outlined against the pale blue eye of northern spring,
Heavily planted in this printed muslin beauty
Of clumps and spots and dots and tiger-stripes,
She swelled with ideas and ideals of duty,
Emphatic,
                Rheumatic.

Mrs. Thatch,
The wife, she was sorry to say,
Of Lord X's gardener
—If such one could call him—
Was silly, town-bred, what Mrs. Hague would call
—Well, she really did not like to say it,
Did not know what to call it;
Shall we say a Ne'er-do-Well?
And all the time the primroses, the wind-flowers
Opened their eyes and pressed their nodding heads

Against her, and the moss seemed ready to
Run up those rugged limbs,
The lichen ready
To crystallize its feathery formations
Along these solid branches.

If not upon this flower-sprinkled mound,
Then Mrs. Hague stood
Pressed in the narrow framework of her door,
And fills it to our minds for evermore.
Out of the slender gaps
Between the figure and its frame,
Was wafted the crusty, country odour
Of new bread,
Which was but one blossom of the hedges
That Mrs. Hague had planted.

For Mrs. Hague was childless,
And so had wisely broken up her life
With fences of her own construction,
Above which she would peer
With bovine grace,
Kind nose, kind eyes
Wide open in wide face.
For
   Monday was Washing Day,
   Tuesday was Baking Day,
   Wednesday h'Alfred 'as 'is dinner h'early,
   Thursday was Baking Day again,
   Friday was a busy day, a very busy day,
   And Saturday prepared the way for Sunday,
   Black satin bosoms and a brooch,
   A bonnet and a Bible.

Nor were these all:
There were other more imposing barriers
Of Strawberry Jam in June
And Blackberry Jelly in October:
For each fruit contributed a hedge
To the garden of Mrs. Hague's days.

These fences made life safe for Mrs. Hague;
Each barrier of washing, mending, baking
Was a barricade
Thrown up against being lonely or afraid.
This infinite perspective
—The week, the month, the year—
Showed in the narrow gaps
Between her and the door,
As she stood there in the doorway,
Narrow as a coffin.

Oh, who can describe the grace of Mrs. Hague,
A Mrs. Noah limned by Botticelli,
'Mid flowering trees, green winds and pensive flowers;
A Rousseau portrait, inflated by Picasso;
Or seen in summer,
As through a tapestry
Of pool, exotic flower and conifer?

As Daphne was transformed into a tree,
So some old elm had turned to Mrs. Hague,
Thick bole, wide arms and rustic dignity.

On the Coast of Coromandel

On the coast of Coromandel
Dance they to the tunes of Handel;
Chorally, that coral coast
Correlates the bone to ghost,
Till word and limb and note seem one,
Blending, binding act to tone.

All day long they point the sandal
On the coast of Coromandel.
Lemon-yellow legs all bare
Pirouette to peruqued air
From the first green shoots of morn,
Cool as northern hunting-horn,
Till the nightly tropic wind
With its rough-tongued, grating rind

Shatters the frail spires of spice.
Imaged in the lawns of rice
(Mirror-flat and mirror green
Is that lovely water's sheen)
Saraband and rigadoon
Dance they through the purring noon,
While the lacquered waves expand
Golden dragons on the sand—
Dragons that must steaming die
From the hot sun's agony—
When elephants, of royal blood,
Plod to bed through lilied mud,
Then evening, sweet as any mango,
Bids them do a gay fandango,
Minuet, jig or gavotte.
How they hate the turkey-trot,
The nautch-dance and the highland fling,
Just as they will never sing
Any music save by Handel
On the coast of Coromandel!

WILFRED OWEN

1893-1918

Strange Meeting

1918

It seemed that out of the battle I escaped
Down some profound dull tunnel, long since scooped
Through granites which titanic wars had groined.
Yet also there encumbered sleepers groaned,
Too fast in thought or death to be bestirred.
Then, as I probed them, one sprang up, and stared
With piteous recognition in fixed eyes,
Lifting distressful hands as if to bless.
And by his smile, I knew that sullen hall,
By his dead smile I knew we stood in Hell.
With a thousand fears that vision's face was grained;
Yet no blood reached there from the upper ground,
And no guns thumped, or down the flues made moan.
'Strange, friend,' I said, 'here is no cause to mourn.'

'None,' said the other, 'save the undone years,
The hopelessness.   Whatever hope is yours,
Was my life also; I went hunting wild
After the wildest beauty in the world,
Which lies not calm in eyes, or braided hair,
But mocks the steady running of the hour,
And if it grieves, grieves richlier than here.
For by my glee might many men have laughed,
And of my weeping something had been left,
Which must die now.   I mean the truth untold,
The pity of war, the pity war distilled.
Now men will go content with what we spoiled,
Or, discontent, boil bloody, and be spilled.
They will be swift with swiftness of the tigress,
None will break ranks, though nations trek from progress.
Courage was mine, and I had mystery,
Wisdom was mine, and I had mastery;
To miss the march of this retreating world
Into vain citadels that are not walled.
Then, when much blood had clogged their chariot-wheels,
I would go up and wash them from sweet wells,
Even with truths that be too deep for taint.
I would have poured my spirit without stint
But not through wounds; not on the cess of war.
Foreheads of men have bled where no wounds were.
I am the enemy you killed, my friend.
I knew you in this dark; for so you frowned
Yesterday through me as you jabbed and killed.
I parried; but my hands were loath and cold.
Let us sleep now. . . .'

THE HON. VICTORIA SACKVILLE-WEST

b. 1892

Orchards

Sometimes in apple country you may see
A ghostly orchard standing all in white,
Aisles of white trees, white branches, in the green,
On some still day when the year hangs between

Winter and spring, and heaven is full of light.
And rising from the ground pale clouds of smoke
Float through the trees and hang upon the air,
Trailing their wisps of blue like a swelled cloak
From the round cheeks of breezes. But though fair
To him who leans upon the gate to stare
And muse 'How delicate in spring they be,
That mobled blossom and that wimpled tree,'
There is a purpose in the cloudy aisles
That took no thought of beauty for its care.
For here's the beauty of all country miles,
Their rolling pattern and their space:
That there's a reason for each changing square,
Here sleeping fallow, there a meadow mown,
All to their use ranged different each year,
The shaven grass, the gold, the brindled roan,
Not in some search for empty grace,
But fine through service and intent sincere.

From *The Land*

EDMUND BLUNDEN

b. 1896

The Idlers

The gipsies lit their fires by the chalk-pit gate anew,
And the hoppled horses supped in the further dusk and dew;
The gnats flocked round the smoke like idlers as they were
And through the goss and bushes the owls began to churr.

An ell above the woods the last of sunset glowed
With a dusky gold that filled the pond beside the road;
The cricketers had done, the leas all silent lay,
And the carrier's clattering wheels went past and died away.

The gipsies lolled and gossiped, and ate their stolen swedes,
Made merry with mouth-organs, worked toys with piths of
    reeds:
The old wives puffed their pipes, nigh as black as their hair,
And not one of them all seemed to know the name of care.

The Barn

Rain-sunken roof, grown green and thin
For sparrows' nests and starlings' nests;
Dishevelled eaves; unwieldy doors,
Cracked rusty pump, and oaken floors,
And idly-pencilled names and jests
      Upon the posts within.

The light pales at the spider's lust,
The wind tangs through the shattered pane:
An empty hop-poke spreads across
The gaping frame to mend the loss
And keeps out sun as well as rain,
      Mildewed with clammy dust.

The smell of apples stored in hay
And homely cattle-cake is there.
Use and disuse have come to terms,
The walls are hollowed out by worms,
But men's feet keep the mid-floor bare
      And free from worse decay.

Almswomen

At Quincey's moat the squandering village ends,
And there in the almshouse dwell the dearest friends
Of all the village, two old dames that cling
As close as any true-loves in the spring.
Long, long ago they passed threescore-and-ten,
And in this doll's house lived together then;
All things they have in common, being so poor,
And their one fear, Death's shadow at the door.
Each sundown makes them mournful, each sunrise
Brings back the brightness in their failing eyes.
How happy go the rich fair-weather days
When on the roadside folk stare in amaze
At such a honeycomb of fruit and flowers
As mellows round their threshold; what long hours

They gloat upon their steepling hollyhocks,
Bee's balsams, feathery southernwood, and stocks,
Fiery dragons'-mouths, great mallow leaves
For salves, and lemon-plants in bushy sheaves,
Shagged Esau's-hands with fine green finger-tips.
Such old sweet names are ever on their lips.
As pleased as little children where these grow
In cobbled pattens and worn gowns they go,
Proud of their wisdom when on gooseberry shoots
They stuck eggshells to fright from coming fruits
The brisk-billed rascals; pausing still to see
Their neighbour owls saunter from tree to tree,
Or in the hushing half-light mouse the lane
Long-winged and lordly.
               But when those hours wane
Indoors they ponder, scared by the harsh storm
Whose pelting saracens on the window swarm,
And listen for the mail to clatter past
And church clock's deep bay withering on the blast;
They feed the fire that flings a freakish light
On pictured kings and queens grotesquely bright,
Platters and pitchers, faded calendars
And graceful hour-glass trim with lavenders.

Many a time they kiss and cry, and pray
That both be summoned in the selfsame day,
And wiseman linnet tinkling in his cage
End too with them the friendship of old age,
And all together leave their treasured room
Some bell-like evening when the may's in bloom.

ROY CAMPBELL

1902-5

Autumn

I love to see when leaves depart,
The clear anatomy arrive,
Winter, the paragon of art,
That kills all forms of life and feeling
Save what is pure and will survive.

Already now the clanging chains
Of geese are harnessed to the moon:
Stripped are the great sun-clouding planes:
And the dark pines, their own revealing,
Let in the needles of the noon.

Strained by the gale the olives whiten
Like hoary wrestlers bent with toil
And, with the vines, their branches lighten
To brim our vats where summer lingers
In the red froth and sun-gold oil.

Soon on our hearth's reviving pyre
Their rotted stems will crumble up:
And like a ruby, panting fire,
The grape will redden on your fingers
Through the lit crystal of the cup.

The Serf

His naked skin clothed in the torrid mist
That puffs in smoke around the patient hooves,
The ploughman drives, a slow somnambulist,
And through the green his crimson furrow grooves.
His heart, more deeply than he wounds the plain,
Long by the rasping share of insult torn,
Red clod, to which the war-cry once was rain
And tribal spears the fatal sheaves of corn,
Lies fallow now.   But as the turf divides
I see in the slow progress of his strides
Over the toppled clods and falling flowers,
The timeless, surly patience of the serf
That moves the nearest to the naked earth
And ploughs down palaces, and thrones, and towers.

CECIL DAY LEWIS

b. 1905

A Time to Dance

For those who had the power
  of the forest fires that burn
Leaving their source in ashes
  to flush the sky with fire:
Those whom a famous urn
  could not contain, whose passion
Brimmed over the deep grave
  and dazzled epitaphs:
For all that have won us wings
  to clear the tops of grief,
My friend who within me laughs
  bids you dance and sing.

Some set out to explore
  earth's limit, and little they recked if
Never their feet came near it
  outgrowing the need for glory:
Some aimed at a small objective
  but the fierce updraught of their spirit
Forced them to the stars.
  Are honoured in public who built
The dam that tamed a river;
  or holding the salient for hours
Against odds, cut off and killed,
  are remembered by one survivor.

All these. But most for those
  whom accident made great,
As a radiant chance encounter
  of cloud and sunlight grows
Immortal on the heart:
  whose gift was the sudden bounty
Of a passing moment, enriches
  the fulfilled eye for ever.

Their spirits float serene
  above time's roughest reaches,
But their seed is in us and over
  our lives they are evergreen.

The Ecstatic

Lark, skylark, spilling your rubbed and round
Pebbles of sound in air's still lake,
Whose widening circles fill the noon; yet none
Is known so small beside the sun:

Be strong your fervent soaring, your skyward air!
Tremble there, a nerve of song!
Float up there where voice and wing are one,
A singing star, a note of light!

Buoyed, embayed in heaven's noon-wide reaches—
For soon light's tide will turn—Oh stay!
Cease not till day streams to the west, then down
That estuary drop down to peace.

MARTYN SKINNER

b. 1906

One Man, symbolic of his Native Land

Alex.   Then came Dunkirk to mitigate the news:
One of those names like Blenheim's, Waterloo's,
Which suddenly Fame in its file writes down;
Unknown one year, the next for ever known.
How close to miracle seemed that retreat;
As if, by some blest providential cheat,
Victory had been defeated by defeat,
The winged eluded by the broken-winged!
Yet still our coasts with hazards huge were ringed,
Waiting to strike.   For France was prostrate then,
And France's victor marshalling his men

O

To give his victory its final form.
Eerie the hush in England ere the storm:
Still skies, the stillness heralding disaster;
And one man's voice, the situation's master.
One man, whose very blemishes seemed great;
Whose life, had Rome not England been his state,
Plutarch had loved to write, and North translate;
Who time on time in those dumbfounding days
Rallied his country round a famous phrase,
Opposing to the other's frenzied fit
Calm eloquence and chuckle-stirring wit;
For not alone with Nazis was his feud,
Stern foe to Hitler—and to platitude.
  Martyn. For that the poet blesses him indeed—
A minister whose speeches men could read—
But benediction's due for more than that,
The massive head beneath the curious hat,
Exuberant, pugnacious, puckish, bland,
Appeared symbolic of his native land,
As typical of England as its pleasures,
Its poetry, its turf, its weights and measures;
And by such native greatness were we shown
That, isolated, we were not alone:
The glories of our past were our allies;
The Armada had but shifted to the skies;
Churchill was now what Drake and Pitt were then.
Hitler one more of History's wicked men.

From *Letters to Malaya*, III and IV

WYSTAN HUGH AUDEN

b. 1907

Look, Stranger

Look, stranger, at this island now
The leaping light for your delight discovers,
Stand stable here
And silent be,

That through the channels of the ear
May wander like a river
The swaying sound of the sea.

Here at the small field's ending pause
Where the chalk wall falls to the foam, and its tall ledges
Oppose the pluck
And knock of the tide,
And the shingle scrambles after the sucking surf, and the gull
    lodges
A moment on its sheer side.

Far off like floating seeds the ships
Diverge on urgent voluntary errands;
And the full view
Indeed may enter
And move in memory as now these clouds do,
That pass the harbour mirror
And all the summer through the water saunter.

O what is that Sound

O what is that sound which so thrills the ear
   Down in the valley drumming, drumming?
Only the scarlet soldiers, dear,
   The soldiers coming.

O what is that light I see flashing so clear
   Over the distance brightly, brightly?
Only the sun on their weapons, dear,
   As they step lightly.

O what are they doing with all that gear;
   What are they doing this morning, this morning?
Only the usual manœuvres, dear,
   Or perhaps a warning.

O why have they left the road down there;
   Why are they suddenly wheeling, wheeling?
Perhaps a change in the orders, dear;
   Why are you kneeling?

O*

O haven't they stopped for the doctor's care;
    Haven't they reined their horses, their horses?
Why, they are none of them wounded, dear,
    None of these forces.

O is it the parson they want with white hair;
    Is it the parson, is it, is it?
No, they are passing his gateway, dear,
    Without a visit.

O it must be the farmer who lives so near;
    It must be the farmer so cunning, so cunning?
They have passed the farm already, dear,
    And now they are running.

O where are you going? stay with me here!
    Were the vows you swore me deceiving, deceiving?
No, I promised to love you, dear,
    But I must be leaving.

O it's broken the lock and splintered the door,
    O it's the gate where they're turning, turning;
Their feet are heavy on the floor
    And their eyes are burning.

LOUIS MACNEICE

b. 1907

Snow

The room was suddenly rich and the great bay-window was
Spawning snow and pink roses against it
Soundlessly collateral and incompatible:
World is suddener than we fancy it.

World is crazier and more of it than we think,
Incorrigibly plural. I peel and portion
A tangerine and spit the pips and feel
The drunkenness of things being various.

And the fire flames with a bubbling sound for world
Is more spiteful and gay than one supposes—
On the tongue on the eyes on the ears in the palms of one's
    hands—
There is more than glass between the snow and the huge roses.

STEPHEN SPENDER

b. 1909

The Express

After the first powerful plain manifesto
The black statement of pistons, without more fuss
But gliding like a queen, she leaves the station.
Without bowing and with restrained unconcern
She passes the houses which humbly crowd outside,
The gasworks and at last the heavy page
Of death, printed by gravestones in the cemetery.
Beyond the town there lies the open country
Where, gathering speed, she acquires mystery,
The luminous self-possession of ships on ocean.
It is now she begins to sing—at first quite low
Then loud, and at last with a jazzy madness—
The song of her whistle screaming at curves,
Of deafening tunnels, brakes, innumerable bolts.
And always light, aerial, underneath
Goes the elate metre of her wheels.
Steaming through metal landscape on her lines
She plunges new eras of wild happiness
Where speed throws up strange shapes, broad curves
And parallels clean like the steel of guns.
At last, further than Edinburgh or Rome,
Beyond the crest of the world, she reaches night
Where only a low streamline brightness
Of phosphorus on the tossing hills is white.
Ah, like a comet through flame she moves entranced
Wrapt in her music no bird song, no, nor bough
Breaking with honey buds, shall ever equal.

elate = triumphant, rhythmical beat.

ALEX COMFORT

b. 1920

Third Elegy

Tree of the hillside, Apple tree,
high in the morning
drop your red apples.

The shadows of birds and their small bright mouths
leap over woods that part the bending rivers—
over the creeping ridges, valley to valley
the spires of cockcrow and the cold bell answer
far to the blind sea, to the drowned ledges;
spanned by the sky's wide beaches.   Or fine spires
the gold birds flash swinging above the copses
and out of farms under the intricate sky
the tall necks yell incessant at the morning—

among your leaves of the fountain
a hundred reddening globes, the faces of children
tree of the chalk hill, Apple tree
roll your red apples to the parishes;
down to wet valleys, by streams, hung with the leaves' old faces.

The faces of birds clash on the sharp beaks of the dead.
Those leaping spears that drive the graveyards home
into the spongy hills, restore the pattern
of crops and the order of fields, and the roads run over
the road-builders, and the quilts of corn
cover cold farmers.   But the sharp sad faces
the skulls of killed sheep, the staring cups
robbed long of gold and bitter eyes
lie in white outposts on the hills' brown lid.
Hollow stones, scattered in windy places
on the high moors, no spire or cockcrow reaches.

Tree of the hillside, Apple tree—
whom no lid deceives, whose slim roots wander
the brown cells of the hill, caressed
by hard, quick fingers that have forgotten apples
that have forgotten the skill of the harrow, the old
skill of the crooked roads and the flight of herons
that have forgotten the long and bitter barrow
cast your bright faces, children's sorrowless faces.

O poet, hillside tree, O swift combiner
of the sad hunters' messages tapped in the dark hill
into the upgoing song of leaves and the red
cold falling faces of your pure children
fountain voice, taught by the voiceless faces
show me your knowledge—cast your happy fruit.

The cocks ride swinging, over the brown male voices:
but always under the fields, battened and locked
grey mouths instruct me that have forgotten lips—
the hatches move as I walk over them,
always the beggars, the bereft, through the bars of the fields
call me, plead for my voice, for my voice, to borrow it,
and I am dumb to fling the mumbled sign
the glimpsed deep woods, the sound of tusk and horn
and the long arrow flying down the years
up to the deep sky, into the singing fountain.

O apple tree
O green interpreter
distil this tossing sorrow
into your red timeless apples. . . .

Now after cockcrow on the populous hills
we stand between the living and the sharp
beseeching faces, pressing from the earth
their urchin heads to the cloudy panes of the grass
apple tree, upright speaker, deliverer
of these red perfect warnings, give me your courage.
When I am silent, I can hear the teeth
gnash in the blind hill. I am ambassador

unwilling of so many.   Teach me to live
a speaking fountain for the tongueless faces.

Teach me acceptance.
I did not choose them
Even in childhood there were hands that plucked at my feet.

Apple tree, tree of the hillside
down on the riding spires, for tears
toss your red apples.

INDEX OF AUTHORS

INDEX OF FIRST LINES

PRINTED IN GREAT BRITAIN BY NEILL AND CO. LTD., EDINBURGH